1000

Bill Horn

How To Write With A
Collaborator

HAL ZINA BENNETT
with
MICHAEL LARSEN

Writer's
Digest
Books

Cincinnati, Ohio

How to Write with a Collaborator. Copyright © 1988 by Hal Zina Bennett and Michael Larsen. Printed and bound in the United States of America. All rights reserved. No part of this book may be reproduced in any form or by any electronic or mechanical means including information storage and retrieval systems without permission in writing from the publisher, except by a reviewer, who may quote brief passages in a review. Published by Writer's Digest Books, an imprint of F&W Publications, Inc., 1507 Dana Avenue, Cincinnati, Ohio 45207. First edition.

93 92 91 90 89 88   5 4 3 2 1

Library of Congress Cataloging-in-Publication Data

Bennett, Hal Zina, 1936—
  How to write with a collaborator.

  Bibliography: p.
  Includes index.
  1. Authorship—Collaboration.   I. Larsen, Michael.   II. Title.
PN145.B46   1988   808'.02   87-34081
ISBN 0-89879-308-4

Design by Joan Jacobus.

ACKNOWLEDGMENTS

Books are always collaborative efforts. Behind every writer or writing team there are editors, book designers, secretaries, and production people whose names seldom appear in print but whose work is absolutely essential for a book's success.

As authors, we know that it is impossible to thank all of our many collaborators by name. But we do want to say that we have felt the support of the entire staff at Writer's Digest Books, and we want you all to know that your work has been important to us in a thousand ways, large and small.

It has been a great joy to work with all of you.

Special thanks to Jean Fredette who saw the need for a book of this kind, and to Nan Dibble, whose friendship, editorial suggestions, and "reading between the lines" did so much to clarify the final manuscript and make the book easy and fun to read.

We would also like to thank our helpmates, Susan J. Sparrow and Elizabeth Pomada, for their loving support in this project.

CONTENTS

CHAPTER 5

NINE EASY PIECES—BUILDING THE FOUNDATION FOR SUCCESS

Success begins with an idea that impassions you. Ideas—your stock in trade. An idea list to jog your mind. Linking ideas with the right collaborator. Pitfalls, and how to avoid them. Where to find top experts for non-fiction collaborations.

CHAPTER 6

PEOPLE SKILLS—THE KEYS OF PRODUCTIVITY

What you need to know before your first meeting with a potential collaborator. Developing effective people skills that bring out the best in you and your writing partner. Checklists for choosing your collaborator. Differences between fiction and non-fiction collaborations. Checklist of "Dos and Don'ts." Warning signs: how to keep your project on track, or put it back on track if it derails. Systems for dividing responsibilities. Key issues to consider before writing contracts or other working agreements.

CHAPTER 7

AGREEMENTS AND CONTRACTS— DEFINING WORK RELATIONSHIPS

How contracts can help keep your creative energy high and the collaboration exciting and productive. Three forms of contracts that must be considered. Stepped agreements for minimizing the risk of a new collaboration. Sample contracts. The key parts of a proposal to sell a book project to a publisher. Pitfalls to avoid. Who is doing what? The importance of working chapter outlines, and how to write them. How to be your own literary agent. Working with literary agents. Most common questions and answers about agents. What to look for in publishers' contracts. Resource list of literary attorneys.

CHAPTER 8

A WRITER'S WORK IS NEVER DONE

A realistic look at relationships with agents, publishers, editors, and sales people. Responsibilities that extend beyond writing. Following through—from idea, to writing the manuscript, to working with your editor, to checking galley proofs, to book promotion. How to make it all work for you.

COLLABORATIVE WRITING SIMPLIFIED—A ROAD MAP TO SUCCESS

To claim that there is a handful of simple rules you can follow to become a successful collaborator is, of course, misleading. As in becoming a successful poet, novelist, essayist, doctor, lawyer, engineer, or anything else, we each have our own ways of learning and our own ways of integrating the skills we need. Rarely do those things that truly matter in our lives fit into tidy packages. Simplicity is often, as Shakespeare said, "compounded of many simples, extracted from many objects, and indeed the sundry contemplation of my travels."

In spite of this, we have developed the following fifteen subject areas to give you a broad picture of what you'll need to achieve success in your collaboration. Not intended as a step-by-step plan, these points nevertheless provide the road map for reaching your goal.

1. *Explore Pros and Cons.* Read this book to learn about the advantages and disadvantages of collaboration, and decide if this way of writing is the right way for you.

2. *Match Working Styles to Fit Your Needs.* Become knowledgeable about the various kinds of collaborative writing arrangements that are possible—from ghostwriting to coauthorship—so that you can choose the one that best suits your personal temperament, your financial needs, and the scope of the project you're considering.

1

3. *Be True to Yourself.* Find an idea that you feel passionate about. Take the initiative, whether you are the writer looking for an expert or celebrity with whom to work, or the expert or celebrity looking for a writer. Your initiative will help motivate others in any project you're involved with.

4. *Clarify Your Ideas.* Research and develop your idea so that you can present it in an exciting way to people you are considering for a writing collaboration.

5. *Seek Out a Collaborator.* This could be through visiting or becoming a member of civic groups, professional groups, writers' clubs, celebrity gatherings, etc., where you are most likely to connect with the people who can fill your needs.

6. *Test the Waters.* Before making long-term commitments, get to know your collaborator with a series of meetings and "stepped agreements" (see pages 92-93) that assure you both that you can work together harmoniously.

7. *Learn People Skills.* Develop a kit of "people skills" for keeping your collaboration productive and personally satisfying. Collaborations, like friendships and marriages, require attention to personal needs beyond the craft of writing.

8. *Conceptualize and Plan.* Work with your collaborator to develop your idea for a selling proposal. Begin writing chapter outlines and sample chapters for the proposal. If you are working on a book of fiction, write a book outline and sample chapters that you can show to agents or publishers. Share your work with friends to get feedback. Note that agents and editors require a complete novel manuscript, whereas nonfiction can be sold with a proposal and sample chapters.

9. *Find an Agent or Publisher.* See Appendix F for resources that will help you locate these.

10. *Submit a Professional-looking Proposal or Manuscript.* The appearance of your proposal or manuscript reflects the professionalism with which you are approaching the subject and your career. Your proposal must look and read like it's worth the advance you want for it. Start with a phone call or query letter. Follow up with an attractively presented proposal or manuscript with an SASE for its return.

11. *Sell the Book.* With or without an agent, it is up to you to convince the publisher that your book will be a worthwhile or profitable project.

12. *Negotiate.* Work out a publishing contract that is fair to both collaborators.

13. *Write the Book.* If you have accomplished all of the above, writing the book should go smoothly and be a satisfying experience for both of you.

14. *Promote the Book.* Promoting the book may involve one or both authors.

15. *Replay.* In an ideal collaboration, you develop and submit the proposal for your next book together while you are still writing the first one. By the time your first manuscript has been accepted, you should be receiving the first half of your advance to start the next book.

With this road map in mind, we welcome you to the exciting prospect of your first writing collaboration. Whether you are: a writer working with another writer; a writer working with an expert or celebrity; an expert or celebrity working with a writer; an editor, an agent, or a publisher seeking the best way to put together a successful collaborative project; this book will help.

At their best, collaborations are like perfect marriages. The partnership turns out to have the right chemistry or magic that creates something new, something much larger than the sum of its parts. Out of the union comes a third voice, previously unknown to those whose efforts were responsible for it. It is almost as if, through working together, a new mind that generates ideas and a distinctive new voice are born that neither author could have created alone.

In the pages ahead, you'll be reading about some of the most successful collaborations the publishing world has known. It is our hope that this book, itself a collaboration, will provide the *alchemy* you need to reap the greatest literary and financial rewards the writing profession has to offer.

2

MINING THE TREASURES OF COLLABORATION

How can you make 1 + 1 equal $1 million? You can do it in publishing and other media by teaming up with another writer, or with a noted authority, a researcher, a public figure, an illustrator, or a photographer. Consider the following works: *Iacocca* and *In Search of Excellence,* in nonfiction; *The Talisman,* in fiction; *Auntie Mame,* in playwriting; *Top Gun,* in film; *Mr. Halley and His Comet,* in children's books; and *Cosmos,* in science. All these works have two things in common: first, they were all best-sellers, with most earning more than $1 million for their authors; and second, they were all collaborations.

These are not isolated cases. A list of successful collaborations would fill the pages of a book twice this size. Successful collaborations embrace every genre: poetry, romance novels, scholarly works, technical manuals for software producers, academic theses, textbooks, and expensive "coffee-table" art books. Virtually everywhere that words are used we find collaborations.

Every year, millions of dollars in advances and royalties are earned by collaborative writers, many of whom have never been published. These earnings are sometimes being shared with people who don't write at all, but who have something important or exciting to tell us. The opportunities for writers who can collaborate with other writers, with celebrities, or with experts who don't have the time, ability, or inclination to write, are greater than ever before.

In spite of the evidence that collaboration can be a highly

profitable field, few people are taking advantage of it. Every year, there are thousands of book projects looking for good writers, projects that promise good pay for freelancers who can collaborate. A great many of these book projects have all the ingredients for success except one: the people with the story, or with the expertise, or with the public acclaim can't write. This creates a high-earning publishing niche for writers who are capable of shaping books from other people's material.

Providing the writing skills for a book project is just one kind of collaboration. You have only to look at the best-seller lists to realize that something new is happening in the collaborative writing field. Collaboration is becoming an art form in itself, and it is one that opens up possibilities that have never been available before to so many writers.

Maybe you are a person who has dreamed for years of writing a book. Maybe you have a desk drawer full of notes outlining scenes or characters or plots if you're a fiction writer, or ideas and resources if your interest is nonfiction. You know you have a book in you but somehow there's a missing ingredient. You know how to create intriguing characters for a novel—but you are lost when it comes to developing a plot. Or you are a fine researcher—but you can't even begin to imagine how to organize the research for a book.

Writers are collecting handsome royalties for books that, without a collaborator, they would never have been able to develop. There are people whose dreams of becoming published writers—in fiction, nonfiction, theater, film, and technical areas—became realities when they teamed up with others whose interests, and perhaps frustrations, complemented their own. Their lives were transformed when they discovered the opportunities that collaboration provides. You will be reading about such people and about the variety of possible collaborations.

Some of the most successful writers in the world depend on one form of collaboration or another. Let your mind entertain all kinds of possibilities. For example, the "collaborator" might be a secretary who transcribes and edits after the author tells the story aloud, recording it on a tape recorder. Such is the case with Barbara Cartland, the queen of the romance novel industry. She has authored over 200 books that way. With 350 million copies of her books in print, few people in publishing can match her pace. Legend has it that she can dictate up to 7,000 words a day, and even in her 80s, she and her collaborative team wrote 30,000 words per week.

Collaborations between writers who are accomplished in their own right are not unusual. Did you know, for example, that Edmund Wilson and F. Scott Fitzgerald once collaborated on writing a play? More recently, we have seen collaborations between well-established writers such as Stephen King and Peter Straub, who produced *The Talisman*. The team-up between partners Jim Cash and John Epps, Jr., who produced the film scripts for *Top Gun* and *Legal Eagles,* suggests that there is an appeal about this form of writing that transcends raw necessity. Jerome Lawrence and Robert E. Lee, who wrote over twenty major plays—including *Inherit the Wind* and *Auntie Mame*—in their long history as collaborators, say that there is a magic about working together that can't be duplicated by working alone. Like many writers who collaborate, they feel that the "ultimate product of the collaboration is much larger than the sum of its parts."

Not only famous writers are opting for writing collaborations. There are plenty of books by lesser-known writers who, sometimes unknown to their readers, have always written as a team. Examples? In the romance genre, the writing team of Sharon and Tom Curtis write under the pseudonym of Robin James, while a team of three—Jean Harvey, Tina MacKenzie and Laura Bennett—wrote the genre novel *Memory And Desire* under the pseudonym Justine Harlowe.

In the children's book field, one of the most interesting collaborations is the one that grew between Teresa and Raf Dahlquist. This husband and wife team has developed a series of whimsical, illustrated books about famous scientists. Raf is the scientist, the researcher for this team, while Teresa generates ideas and writes the prose. Their first successful book together was *Mr. Halley And His Comet.*

The new brand of collaborative writer has replaced what the publishing world once referred to as "ghosts." A ghost was the silent partner of a celebrity or authority. Although ghosts did the writing, usually for a flat fee, their names rarely appeared on the cover. If they were lucky, there might be a mention in the acknowledgements, with a tag line such as "for help with the manuscript."

Although the need for ghostwriters still exists, the new breed of collaboration often involves people who in their own right may be gifted novelists, playwrights, essayists, or poets. Unlike ghostwriters, they frequently get author credits and usually share in the royalties. They are highly respected in the industry, both for the work they do in coauthorships and for the work they do on their own.

NEW PRECEDENTS IN PUBLISHING

In the past few years as a literary agent, Michael has watched collaborative writers gain a new place in publishing, becoming the silent heroes and heroines of the industry. You may or may not see their names on the book jackets they coauthor, or if you see them, theirs are not the ones you remember. Instead, you recall names like Lee Iacocca, Chuck Yeager, or Priscilla Presley, just three of the hundreds of people for whom editors seek collaborative writers every year.

Do the names William Novak, or Leo Janos, or Sandra Harmon leap out at you? Unless you're in the book business, the answer is no. Yet these are the people who did the writing for those three best-selling authors just mentioned.

William Novak's success story is a good example. Although he had published three nonfiction books on his own, he had given up hope of ever making a living as an author. Then an editor friend asked if he'd consider working on a memoir with Lee Iacocca. Novak agreed and the rest is history. The book he wrote with the man who saved the Chrysler Corporation rose quickly on the best-seller lists, eventually to top 2.5 million in hardcover sales. And another Iacocca book is in the works.

Novak received a $45,000 flat fee for his work on this phenomenally successful book, with an additional $35,000 bonus. In contracts he has signed since then, including a book with Herb Schmertz, the vice-president of Mobil Oil, his agent has made certain that Novak gets a percentage of the royalties.

The success of the Iacocca book is a real glamour story, one that has given the collaborative writer a big boost in the publishing world. This book, along with a half dozen others, has altered the concept of writers who produce books for people who either can't write or don't have the time to write themselves. The term "ghostwriter" has been replaced by "collaborator" or even "co-author." This change is not pure rhetoric, but reflects a significant rise in the status of the collaborating writer.

There was a time when people wouldn't admit that their books had been ghosted. The names of their writers, and often even the fact that they had writers, were closely guarded secrets. Likewise, the writers who did this work all too often were hacks who worked for a flat fee, participated only minimally in the shaping of the book, and had very little interest in the eventual outcome of their efforts, once they had fulfilled their end of the bargain. Editors were hard-pressed to get serious writers to consider a collaboration, because better writers thought it beneath their dignity. That is changing as writers find a new challenge in the special relationships that can be established between themselves and their sometimes famous coauthors. Examples of this new dignity in the collaborative relationship abound.

Over twenty years ago a writer acquaintance of ours collaborated on a book with a man who had risen to prominence in the national political arena. In the process of working on that book together, these two people, from seemingly totally different worlds, became lifelong friends. Their mutual respect led to a continuing intellectual dialogue that helped enrich and expand the careers of both men. Those two men's names: writer Orville Schell and California's ex-governor Jerry Brown.

Ben Franklin once wrote, "Either write things worth reading, or do things worth the writing." Here is the formula for successful writing partnerships—one person whose actions are of interest to readers, and one person whose writing can shape those actions into a book that will capture the interest of the book-buying public.

Gone are the days when good writers considered it demeaning to ghost books for celebrities or experts. Changes in the publishing world have brought this about. For one thing, celebrity books have changed. They are no longer a self-aggrandizing indulgence on the part of an actor or captain of industry or expert whose name appears on the cover. Such books now have meat in them.

In big business, figures like Lee Iacocca have become national heroes, and people want to know more about them: what kind of people they are off the job; how they got where they are today; what plans they have for the future.

Collaborative writing offers the opportunity to interact with exciting public figures and celebrities. Since the book-buying public now demands that such books have substance, first-rate professional writers are more than ever attracted to collaborations.

GETTING STARTED

Collaborations are often born in the offices of literary agents or editors. But there are no hard rules here. As a collaborative writer, you can initiate a project and find an expert or a celebrity whose name or expertise will help sell the book, first to an editor and then to the public.

Hal's first collaboration came about because of an idea he got while recuperating in the hospital following a traffic accident. During his hospital stay, he observed that most people are poorly equipped to cope with the scores of medical decisions they face during a serious illness or injury. Hal was convinced that people failed to take part in the medical decisions that affected them not because they were inherently irresponsible about their health care, but because they simply didn't know what to ask. He thought there was a book in this and that people would welcome medical information that was written in a straightforward, nonthreatening way.

As good as the idea sounded, there was one glaring flaw. Hal wasn't a doctor. He wasn't even a health educator. And he had no intention of pursuing careers in these fields for the purpose of writing a book. Still, he believed in the idea, even though the editors he queried said they would consider it only if the book could have an M.D. on the cover.

Hal put his concept for the medical book on a back burner, turning to other writing in the meantime. He was confident that this idea was a good one and that a solution would eventually present itself. Nearly five years passed before anything happened with his brainchild. Then he had a chance meeting with a woman whose husband was a physician, a man who had enjoyed writing in college but whose main interest now was health education. He had a book idea similar to Hal's. The doctor, Mike Samuels, and Hal were introduced, and they became fast friends. In the months that followed, they produced *The Well Body Book,* which sold a quarter of a million copies, was excerpted in major magazines, and was published in six languages. That book paid the rent for both collaborators' families for more than a decade!

The story of how Michael and Hal came to write the book you hold in your hands is perhaps even more characteristic of the way collaborations are formed. Michael and Hal had known each other for many years, both of them being active members in the San Francisco book scene. Both had done workshops for writers in the area—Michael on how to get published, and Hal on collaborations.

One afternoon, during a phone call, Michael asked Hal if he had ever considered writing a book on the subject of collaborations. Surprisingly, Hal hadn't. In his workshops, he had always focused on the personal aspects of that business—how to choose and maintain a productive and creative working relationship. A book, he thought, should be much broader than that. It should include information about contracts and agreements, the business end of publishing that he had always left to his agent.

A bright new collaboration was born at that moment. What better combination for such a book than an experienced collaborator and a successful literary agent who had written books himself and, as an agent, had helped set up numerous collaborations for other writers.

When you begin thinking of yourself as a collaborative writer, new vistas open up to you. The realization that you are not an expert on a subject for a book that you are sure will sell a million copies no longer stops you. You needn't be an expert, except in your writing.

Do you want to write about health? Team up with a health

professional, preferably one with an established name that will help sell your book. Hal wrote four successful books on medical subjects this way.

Are you certain that you have a brilliant book idea concerning astronomy, even though you don't even own a telescope? Team up with the astronomer who lectures at the local planetarium. Consider the record of Carl Sagan, author of *Cosmos,* and his collaborator Ann Druyan. Druyan, Sagan's writer, and the author of several books of her own, stayed in the background for many years. In their recent books, Druyan's name has not only appeared with Carl's on the cover, but their biographies reveal that they are married.

Do you want to write a book exposing political graft? Keep your eyes out for names in the newspapers, for stories of people who have an inside track and a sense of mission about getting their message across.

Do you want to write a book about a famous crime that has received widespread attention? Read the newspaper, then seek out a collaborator from a list of police officials, attorneys, or others whose names appear in the stories. The journalists reporting such stories may also be interested in developing a book with you. Why would another professional writer be interested in collaborating on a book? Newspaper reporting is a different kind of writing from book writing. Besides, the day-to-day responsibilities of staff writers may prevent them from developing a book. With your assistance, they may be able to bridge the gap between their profession and the publication of a book.

One writer, who cannot be named for obvious reasons, was attracted to a news story that told how law enforcement agencies had established a link between organized crime and a certain outlaw motorcycle gang. Working behind the scenes, he established contact with an ex-member of the gang who was under the protection of the FBI. He had regular contacts with this witness, often by phone, and sometimes in strange cities (the FBI moved the witness around as a protective strategy) when the meeting had to be face-to-face.

If you're looking for a tamer way to find a collaborator, at-

tend lectures and workshops given by the hundreds of consultants who make *business* their business. Choose one whose subject
interests you, who is doing well, and who needs a book to increase his or her visibility and credibility. Consider the success of
The One Minute Manager, written by Kenneth Blanchard and
Spencer Johnson, or *In Search Of Excellence,* written by Tom Peters and Robert Waterman.

Open your horizons. Let your mind wander, exploring the
most farfetched possibilities you can entertain. If you're a good
writer, don't limit yourself to those subjects you know well.

Karen Warner, a San Francisco writer, prefers collaboration over writing alone. Her books include *Hollywood Trivia* and
San Francisco Trivia. The latter enjoyed a long run on the *San
Francisco Chronicle*'s Bay Area best-seller list. One day, Michael,
who is her agent, called her up to ask her what she thought she
would like to write next. She said she wasn't sure but she had
been thinking about a cookbook. This telephone call took place
at the restaurant where she worked part-time. After saying
goodbye to Michael, she turned around and arranged the ice
counter in preparation for the dinner crowd. There, staring her
in the face, was the subject and title for her cookbook: OYS-
TERS. Moments later, she was talking with the cook, who agreed
to become her collaborator. Within a week, the book was under
contract.

As the writing half of a collaboration, be enterprising. Put
yourself in a position of control. You are the person with writing
expertise, with the ability to develop proposals, set up collaborations, and make the initial contacts with agents or publishers.
You are offering a valuable service to those thousands of people
whose careers will be boosted by the publication of a book. Establish yourself as a company providing these services—and make
certain you are paid well for your efforts and your expertise.

Remember, you can *hire* your own expert as a collaborator,
in virtually any field. And that expertise not only won't cost you
anything, it may well be your ticket to a handsome advance from
a major publisher, with a continued income from royalties for
many years to come.

HIS, MINE OR OURS?

Hal has worked on more than a dozen collaborative projects, large and small. He has written on education, medicine, death and dying, marriage counseling, business, mental training for athletes, and bicycle riding. He has written children's books, computer books, and books on psychic phenomena.

Of course, he doesn't always collaborate. Many of his books have appeared with just his own name on the cover. But Hal has always allowed his own interests to guide him, never letting himself be limited by his lack of expertise on the subject that captured his imagination.

Michael's collaborations include *Painted Ladies: San Francisco's Resplendent Victorians,* and *Daughters of Painted Ladies: America's Resplendent Victorians*. These photo books about Victorian homes, coauthored with his partner Elizabeth Pomada, presented a special situation, since Michael and Elizabeth also live and work together as agents.

If we have a single piece of advice to share with people considering coauthorships, it is this: Follow your own interests. Choose a writing associate whose interests closely parallel your own. If you don't do this, you might as well go to work writing press releases for a company whose product doesn't interest you. The work will come out flat and uninteresting, and your hours at the typewriter will be drudgery.

STRIKING PAY DIRT

One of the first questions people ask in Hal's workshops on collaborative writing is this: "How difficult is it to sell other people on the idea of teaming up with you?"

In most cases, it's easy. Consider this: People with high visibility—politicians, movie stars, professional athletes, national lecturers, college professors, experts in every field—don't always have time to write their own books. Nor do they usually have the ability. You might think that lecturers would have writing skills, but writing a lecture is different from writing a book.

Hal has collaborated three times with people who were brilliant lecturers. On the podium, they commanded the attention of their audiences, exciting them with laughter one moment, bringing them to the verge of tears the next, and making them think the next. But when it came to putting a book together, these eloquent people were lost. They could stand up and address hundreds of people, and seem to enjoy it. But a blank sheet of paper in the typewriter turned them into cowards. Such people need your help.

Most people in professions where visibility counts know the value of having books with their names on the cover. Lecturers need books to maintain their status on the lecture circuit. Many college professors are expected to produce at least one book every five years. Such books usually aren't on subjects with great commercial promise, but sometimes they are. Carlos Castaneda was an anthropology teacher until his Don Juan series launched him into best-sellerdom. Besides, even those book projects that have only a limited market can help keep bread on the table—and, who knows, in the process of collaborating you may explore a subject you've always wanted to learn.

In today's marketplace, books face growing competition for people's time and money, not just from other books but from other print, broadcast, and electronic media, and from other leisure-time pursuits. Outside of an unpredictable fad like Rubik's Cube, which captured the public's attention, or a book being published at just the right time, the key to a nonfiction book's success is marketing and promotion. And the key to effective promotion is a promotable author. A marketing plan of what the authors will do to promote their books, before and after publication, when the window of opportunity is open to them, is usually the most important part of a book proposal.

National lecturers, celebrities, politicians, and expert consultants have much to offer you in a collaboration. Because they are in the public eye or in demand, such people offer powerful publicity potential, the edge you need to push the book on which you've collaborated onto best-seller lists. When you can combine those assets with your own interest in the subject, you have a winning combination.

THE WORLD'S BEST ADVERTISING

The book business is a peculiar one. And its peculiarities make collaborative writing especially attractive for certain kinds of professional writers. A quick overview of the publishing world will help explain why.

It has been said that no other major industry works on such narrow profit margins. Until recently, most publishing companies were family-run businesses in which turning big profits was not as important as publishing good books. In the past two decades this picture has been changing but some of the mystique remains.

Conglomerates like ABC and RCA and Gulf Western started buying into publishing, starting in the late 1950s and early 1960s. At that point the idealism of the family-run publishers began to take a back seat to the company's "bottom line." This does not mean that the idealism that once drove the publishing industry is dead. Far from it! But that idealism has been tempered by competition and rising costs.

Beginning writers frequently overestimate the money that can be made in this industry. They are dazzled by stories in the press about multimillion-dollar advances and huge advertising budgets. But these stories are exceptions. For every multimillion-dollar contract signed, there are thousands in which authors receive four figures or less—with no advertising budget.

Take a look at some of the hard facts of publishing. It is generally accepted that approximately 50,000 titles are published each year. Of those, about 20,000 are trade books. Of the trade books, nearly 80 percent lose money. Hardcover first printings of 5,000 to 15,000 copies are more the rule than the exception. For trade paperback, a first printing of 10- 20,000 copies is average, with mass market paperback printings in the 50- 100,000 copy range. With authors' royalties ranging from 5 percent of the cover price for mass market paperback to 15 percent of the cover price for hardcover, most writers aren't getting wealthy even if they are the lucky ones who manage to sell out their first printing.

Writers complain that their books don't receive the publicity they deserve. Unless you're a James Michener or Jean Auel in fiction, or a John Naisbitt or Wayne Dyer in nonfiction, your book won't sell enough copies to warrant a large advertising budget. If your book is already selling well, an advertising campaign can help sustain or even increase the sales momentum already there.

Publishing people feel that advertising isn't the chief reason that people buy books. What is? There is no other industry in which word of mouth matters more. If a book offers a "good read," it will win readers regardless of what you do or don't do to promote it. If it's not a good read, no advertising budget will make it a best-seller.

Reading a book is an intimate affair. You can motivate a reader to buy a book, but after getting the book home that reader is going to be spending hours or sometimes days with that purchase. It's those hours while readers are alone with the book that matter. The solitary reader isn't affected by hype. If readers are informed or entertained, they will recommend the book to friends, talk about it at parties and at work, and share insights or anecdotes over lunch with associates. This is the kind of advertising that sells books, and no glossy ad in the world can buy it.

Nevertheless, the book-buying public does need to know that your book is out there. Unless you've got blockbuster material on your hands, the publicity you'll receive for your book will consist of your publisher mailing out a few hundred copies to reviewers, and a mention in *Publishers Weekly*. These efforts may make book sellers aware of your work.

That's the system. Like it or not, it's the best that can be done, given the economic realities of the book business. For writers who invest a year or more of their time producing a book, it can be heart-breaking. However, there are alternatives.

First of all, never forget that the content of your book is its own best advertising. If you've done your job well, and there is a sizable audience interested in the subject or the kind of novel you've written, your book will sell. Satisfied readers will tell their friends, and their friends will tell their friends. That network of referrals is a key to success.

Second, realize that if, in addition to writing, you also have credibility in your field and the ability to get up and speak to groups, to appear on radio and television, and to come across well in newspaper and magazine interviews, there is no better person than you to promote your nonfiction book. However, just as good speakers don't necessarily make good writers, so good writers don't necessarily make good speakers. Writers excel as communicators when they are closed up in a little room with nothing but a telephone, a few of their favorite reference books, a stack of paper, a typewriter or word processor, and maybe a bottle of sherry as insurance against writer's block. For them, mounting the podium is like going to another planet.

Enter the collaborator.

Imagine, if you will, that you are able to produce a book that is a *good read*. You hate speaking to groups, and the fear of getting in front of a television camera is, in your mind, exceeded only by the prospect of facing a firing squad.

However, you have been shrewd enough to marry your writing talents with those of a person who is not only an expert on your joint book's subject but is also a skillful speaker, who enjoys addressing large groups, and who loves everything about the publishing process that you fear. Put that person in front of an audience and the energy generated ripples instantly through the crowd.

In this scenario, you'll have the winning combination that is the dream of every publisher. You produce a good book and your collaborator promotes it.

Given these basic truths, you would ideally choose a person who, in addition to being an expert on the subject of your mutual interest, already makes a good part of his or her living speaking to groups, or otherwise staying in the public eye. Relatively few authors are given publicity tours. But if your subject is current, offering something newsworthy or stimulating for talk shows, publishers will be more likely to ante up money to put you on the road. Typically, a publicity tour means putting the author on the road for two weeks, during which time you will appear on radio and television in a dozen major cities. Hal has done several publicity tours, and they're a blitz—a grueling experience for authors who don't love being in the public eye.

The perfect situation exists when the author can keep the book in the public eye week after week, and month after month. Consider people like Wayne Dyer, whose life is the lecture circuit, or Tom Peters, whose consulting takes him into board rooms of the nation's largest corporations.

SIDESTEPPING CATCHES AND TRAPS

If you think this all sounds too good to be true, you may be right. Collaborative writing takes a special talent. The process of producing a book in this way can be an intimate and trying one. More than once, seasoned book collaborators have compared their associations to marriage. Personal struggles can threaten the bond unless quickly resolved. But also like a marriage, the rewards of a collaboration can be uniquely satisfying.

If writing a nonfiction book is like a marriage, writing the proposal to sell the book idea to a publisher—which we discuss in Chapter Seven—can be like a trial marriage. Preparing such a proposal gives you the chance to prove to yourself, and to each other, that you really do want to do the book, and will enjoy working on it together. If you are going to have a problem with the project, it is far better to discover it before you have signed a contract to write the book.

If you are a fiction writer, your trial marriage will need to be on a slightly different basis, since fiction by new writers is rarely sold on the basis of proposals. Instead, most publishers prefer to see a finished manuscript. The exception to this is published novelists, who may sell their next book on the basis of an outline. If you and your coauthor are fiction writers, write an outline and one or two chapters, before you commit yourself to the whole book.

To succeed as a collaborative writer, you will need people skills in addition to writing skills. If you are the writer, you also need to be able to get your ego out of the way when conflicts arise.

Several years ago, when Hal locked horns with a nationally known lecturer with whom he was working, he turned to a psychologist friend for advice. The psychologist told him: "People who become lecturers and celebrities and the heads of large corporations are not noted for their modesty. In fact, it is their powerful ego needs, and their urgent drive for money, often combined with a sincere sense of mission, that propels them to their exalted positions. They want and they need to have center stage. That's how they get things done. So, above all, never compete with them for that position. They're scrappers, and they've gotten where they are because they know how to defend that little area in center stage where the light is brightest and most flattering and where they know their voices can best be heard."

So, as you consider collaborative writing, remember that in addition to writing skills, it doesn't hurt to be self-effacing, to have expertise in resolving conflicts, and to know how to set limits where your own talents are concerned.

Clear contracts that help define the working relationship are invaluable, but, as in a marriage, you can't count on the words written on the license to maintain the balance. You must like the person with whom you're contracting, and you must trust him or her.

When both parties enter a collaboration with their eyes wide open, having a sense of what to expect, and taking time to develop a close working bond, the relationship can be a chance to explore worlds they might otherwise never encounter. And if you have chosen your ideas and your collaborator well, the economic rewards can exceed your wildest dreams.

In the pages ahead, you will notice that we talk about nonfiction writers more frequently than we speak of fiction writers. The reason for this is that there are many more people collaborating on nonfiction than there are on fiction. Nevertheless, most things we discuss here apply to both kinds of writers. When it doesn't apply, we'll say so.

3

HAUNTING THE GHOST CIRCUIT

This chapter is dedicated to "Anon," the world's most prolific ghost-writer, whose name has been appearing on written works since the beginning of recorded history.

The single thing that distinguishes "ghosts" from collaborative writers may well be that ghosts are more interested in money than fame. Though the books they write may be on best-seller lists, their names are rarely known to the public.

Besides anonymity, there is little to distinguish the ghost from the collaborative writer. Any other contractual terms that apply to collaborations can also be applied to ghosts. For example, if the book is written for a famous person whose name will help sales, the ghostwriter may elect to work on a percentage basis, taking a percentage of the advance against royalties. Ghosts might choose this payment arrangement rather than a flat fee, knowing that in the long run they will have a good chance of earning more money.

Many ghostwriters make certain that they get paid for the hours they spend writing, regardless of whether the manuscript or the proposal actually sells to a publisher. As with any wage earner or contractor, they get paid for their work as they complete it. A contract of this kind is carefully spelled out, so that there can be no ambiguity about the services provided or the money the ghostwriter will receive.

Getting the words down on paper is just one step in writing

a book. Here are some of the other tasks you'll need to undertake:

- Inserting author's revisions and corrections

- Inserting editor's revisions and corrections

- There may be a need to research the material that goes into the book, which can include interviews, library research, and reading, and maybe also the responsibility of negotiating costs and getting releases for the use of copyrighted materials. This work may require travel, telephone calls, correspondence, and arranging payment for the use of long quotations, charts, graphs from other books, etc.

- Artwork may have to be collected from museums or other sources, requiring travel, telephone calls, correspondence, and payment for the use of rights

- As a ghost, you may be responsible for the "back matter" for the book: index and appendices

- Checking "galley proofs," that is, copies of the typeset material from the publisher before books are printed

Professional ghostwriters being paid flat fees should make certain that each responsibility is carefully defined in the contract and that they should contract to do only what they are being paid to do.

As a ghostwriter, think of yourself as a contractor providing specific services, just as a carpenter or plumber or electrician does in the construction of a house. But remember that just as the contractor probably won't get credit on the architect's blueprints, so as a ghostwriter, you should not expect to get author credit on the cover. If you wish to be given credit somewhere in the book, ask for a line in the acknowledgments, thanking you for your work.

LOOKING FOR A GHOST

What if you are an expert looking for a ghost to shape your material into a book? Here, in question and answer form, are the issues you will need to consider.

Q. I have a book idea that I want to develop, but I know nothing about writing. Where might I find a writer that I can hire to work with me?

A. Begin by asking friends and business associates if they know of people who might help you. If you can find someone who has worked with a writer, spend time asking him how his association with that writer worked out. Having that feedback is invaluable. From the same person, you might also get samples of the work they did together.

But what if you can't find a ghostwriter this way? What do you do then?

First and foremost, look for a writer who lives near you, if not in the same town or city, at least in the same state. Unless the project is a simple one—and this means that the ghost only needs to *rewrite* a manuscript that already exists in a more or less complete form—long-distance communication can become costly and cumbersome. Long-distance associations can work, of course, but plan to spend time getting to know each other before signing any contracts. Get together for a face to face meeting. If that's not possible, do it by phone. Mail is third choice.

Look in the Yellow Pages or Business-to-Business Yellow Pages of your phone book. In many cities, particularly in larger metropolitan areas, there's a category for writers. Sometimes it's listed as "Writing Services." That is the obvious place to begin your search for a ghost. Also look in the classified ads of your local newspapers. And, if there is a writer's club or association in your area, attend one of their meetings. How do you find out about such associations? Once again, try the writers' section in the Yellow Pages. Call a listed writer and ask if he or she knows about such associations. Don't say that you're looking for a writer. Just say you're wanting to get into writing and want to make some personal connections with other writers. Alternatively, many writers' groups announce their meetings in the "community calendar" sections of newspapers. Or a creative writing teacher at a local college or university may be able to steer you to a writers' group.

Literary agents are usually a good resource for locating ghostwriters. Often they know of professional writers in all genres, who write their own books or articles but who supplement their income by occasionally writing for others. Once again, check the Yellow Pages for agents near you.

Writers' magazines and networking associations are excellent sources for finding an agent, for advertising to find a ghost, for advertising your services when you are a ghost, and for getting to know writers. Here is a list of some key resources:

WRITER'S DIGEST
1507 Dana Ave.
Cincinnati, OH 45207

THE WRITER
120 Boylston St.
Boston, MA 02116

WEST COAST REVIEW OF BOOKS
1501 N. Hobart Blvd.
Hollywood, CA 90027

WRITERS CONNECTION
1601 Saratoga-Sunnyvale Road, Suite 180
Cupertino, CA 95014

WRITER'S GAZETTE
Trouvere Co. Rt. 2
Box 250
Eclectic, AL 36024

WRITER'S INFO
Rhyme Time/Story Time
Box 2377
Coeur d'Alene, ID 83814

WRITER'S JOURNAL
Lynnmark Publications
Box 2922
Livonia, MI 48150

WRITERS WEST
Box 16097
San Diego, CA 92116

WRITING UPDATE
4812 Folsom Blvd.
Sacramento, CA 95816

Q. How do you evaluate a writer when you find one?

A. Before you interview a single writer, identify the readership for your book. For example, are you aiming your work at a specific professional group or readers interested in, let's say, boat building? After doing this, match the writer to your market. Ask to see samples the writer has produced for the market you wish to reach. If you can't get an exact match, get as close as you can. For example, suppose the ghost you're considering has never produced a manuscript in boat building but has written an article on fine cabinet-making, indicating a general knowledge of allied crafts. Having a writer who doesn't know the subject can be an asset for two reasons: First, because he or she will be more sensitive than you, the expert, about what questions readers unfamiliar with your subject are most likely to ask; and second, the writer will want the same simplicity and clarity in language that a non-expert reading the book will want.

Ask for the name and phone number of a client of the writer's. Then call that person and ask how he or she liked working with the writer. Ghostwriters worth their salt will be glad to put you in touch with such clients.

Look at writing skills first. Then consider how you feel about the person behind the skills. Do you like this person? Is it someone you would enjoy working with? You are hiring him to do a job for you, one that will involve a high degree of personal interaction. You must like or admire the person, and find him or her easy to be with.

When you're considering the personal side of the writer, don't lose sight of basic skill, however. Without the skills, even the nicest person in the world is not going to be able to produce the book for you.

Q. Do all ghostwriters deliver the same services?

A. No. You should be clear about what you need before you go looking for a ghost. The following list should help you clarify what you need:

• I have already produced a complete manuscript but it needs a professional touch—editing and some rewrites.

What you need: a ghost with editing and writing skills.

• I am a pretty decent writer, have published a few articles, but my grammar and spelling are rusty. I think the manuscript is in pretty good shape otherwise.

What you need: a freelance editor more than you need a writer. Look for a person who can do copyediting.

- My writing is grammatically good and I get my ideas down in an organized way, but my writing lacks style and sounds technical or dull.

What you need: a writer who can rewrite your material, a person whose style is lively and interesting.

- I have an idea for a book but don't even know where to begin. My writing experience is limited to scrawled notes on the refrigerator door to my children.

What you need: a professional who has had books published on his or her own, one who can start from scratch and carry you all the way through to the completion of the book. This must also be a person whom you can get along with on a personal basis.

Q. What should I expect to pay?

A. Rates vary from one part of the country to another, as well as from one writer to another. We did a survey of ghosts in four cities who advertised their services in nationally distributed writer's magazines. We asked for "help in rewriting an existing manuscript, one that needs help with organization, style, and grammar." Rates quoted varied from $10 to $120 per hour. Flat fees for a 250-page manuscript varied from $750 to $5,500. A few would not quote figures without seeing the manuscript.

Some ghostwriters were willing to work on a contract basis, getting a small advance on the promise that they would receive a portion of any earned royalties. Such contracts, of course, take us into the world of the collaborator.

Whatever other arrangements you make with your ghostwriter, we recommend that you put together an agreement in which the writer is promised "perks" or bonuses if the book sells. You might, for example, offer a $1,000 bonus if the book gets an advance of $5,000 or more, with another $1,000 bonus if the book sells over 20,000 copies. The main reason for this is that it gives the writer extra motivation to do the best job possible.

A GHOST OF A CHANCE

If you are a ghostwriter, keep in mind that you are running a business, and if you wish to stay in business, you must make certain you are getting paid for the hours you put in. Don't get yourself tied down to a contract where you will get paid only if the book gets an advance from a publisher. Speculating on a book's marketability is risky business. You can write up an agreement that stipulates that you will get perks if the book sells—that is, a bonus of anywhere from $500 to $5,000—but make certain you get paid for the time you put in.

SUMMARY

Strictly speaking, ghostwriters work for flat fees, may or may not get a percentage of the royalties, and do not share in the glory of authorship. This is true even for writers who originate the ideas and produce entire manuscripts on their own.

Originally, ghosts were exactly what the name implies—people whom the public never sees or hears about. In recent years, the term "ghostwriter" has been used more loosely to include what in this book we call "collaborative writers."

JOIN THE ADVENTURE

Sharing the excitement of writing with another person may seem like a strange motive for collaborating, but it may be the most important consideration. Playwright Jerome Lawrence once said of his collaboration with Robert E. Lee: "What turns me on is when Bob and I are working together and we get a line that gives us both goosebumps. That turns me on."

Ordinarily, the isolation and loneliness of the writer's life is a real problem for authors. One must expect to work for weeks or even months, perhaps without feedback from others, never knowing if what one is writing is self-indulgent garbage or the great American novel. It's just the opposite with collaborations, where in most cases feedback can be gotten in a few hours or a few days, depending on the distance between the partners and how they work.

It is the day-to-day, or perhaps more precisely, the moment-to-moment satisfactions of writing that carry you along. So Jerome Lawrence may be right. It is the goosebumps of the well-executed line, shared with a coauthor, that keeps you going. As though to substantiate this point, when asked about the tremendous success he and Lee enjoyed with plays like "Inherit The Wind," Lawrence replied rather offhandedly: "I think we never believed in our success."

The success of this team's collaboration is based on a rare combination of talents. But even more than the partners' perspectives was that they enjoyed each other's creative company. This doesn't mean they were always in agreement. On the contrary, Lee said that the reason that he and Jerome flourished as a team is "partly that we're different. Jerry's viewpoint is often considerably at odds with mine, but who wants a partner who just says yes to everything?"

In response to this comment, Lawrence laughed and remarked: "If he said yes to me all the time, I wouldn't give him 50 percent of my money."

Another author, Michael A. Banks, who collaborates with as many as four different writers on different projects at the same time, states that it is often true that "two heads are better than one." Banks said of his collaboration with Dean Lambe on a science fiction novel, "Each of us is constantly spotting holes in plot, background, characterization, and other areas. Alone, we would doubtless find these problems, but it would take longer and we might not handle them as well."

FREE HELP

Few people have ever heard of Jim Cash and Jack Epps Jr., though the films they have written have played in first run movie houses across the country. Their films include *Legal Eagles,* with Robert Redford and Debra Winger, and *Top Gun,* a film that made a star of Tom Cruise and brought in nearly $200 million in 1986.

In addition to their phenomenal success as a writing team, Cash and Epps are distinguished by another peculiarity in their work style. They live 2,000 miles apart, Epps in Los Angeles, Cash in East Lansing, Michigan. While Epps writes full time, and has sold scripts to major television series such as "Hawaii Five-O," "Kojak," and others, Cash teaches at Michigan State University.

Only rarely do the two writers get together in the same room to write. Instead, they communicate by telephone, mail, and computer modem. Epps is a tenacious researcher, and more often than not his research is in the form of firsthand experience. He is not above putting himself into precarious, or even life-threatening situations if he feels that is what he needs to do to bring a sense of reality to the script.

For *Top Gun,* a story about fighter pilots, Epps really went out on a limb. He rode in jet fighter planes, subjecting himself to the kinds of mental and physical challenges that every pilot entering the Air Force training program must face. At supersonic speeds, he was taken through rolls and dives that tested his outer limits. He struggled against blackouts and the loss of equilibrium that pilots must conquer before they graduate from the training program.

Those who have seen the film may recall the scenes in which pilot recruits were strapped into a bucket seat like those found in the airplanes they hoped to fly. Simulating the situation they would have to face when being ejected from the cockpit of their crippled aircraft over water, they were thrust into a swimming pool at high speed, with a contraption that looked like a high-tech upgrade of a medieval torture device. After hitting the water and sinking to the bottom of the pool, the recruit had to hold his breath for twenty seconds while releasing himself from the straps, safety helmet, and other encumbrances of the *escape capsule*. Epps put himself through this experience three times, before he fully mastered the method for "exiting in an orderly fashion," as it is described in Navy jargon.

Epps uses his passion for first-hand experience both to bring credibility and drama to the script, and to develop intriguing story lines based on the lives of real people he contacts in the process of collecting information. In the Cash-Epps team, it is Epps who develops the stories while Cash, the college professor and family man, writes the dialogue.

Like other successful writing teams, Epps and Cash describe their collaboration in almost mystical terms: Epps describes it as a "word-and-music" relationship, with Cash providing the words and Epps the music. In reply to a question about how they resolve conflicts between them, Cash confided that out of their "two strong egos" they have created a third ego who "knows more than either of us alone." He adds, "The nice thing is, we don't have to pay [this] third person."

ALL IN THE FAMILY

Although they present an entirely different set of problems, husband-and-wife teams are often motivated and held together by the partners' basic enjoyment of each other's company, which may be what brought them together in the first place. Husband-and-wife teams also talk about having common interests in the subject matter, or they say that it is a combination of their interest in the subject matter and their enjoyment of each other's company that makes their collaboration work.

One couple, Judith Barnard and Michael Fain, write under the single pen name of Judith Michael. Their two successful novels, *Deceptions* and *Private Affairs*, firmly established them as a top writing team. Judith and Michael had been together for a number of years before they began writing together. They admit to a certain naivete about making the move to become collaborators. Said Judith, "In the five years we'd been together, we'd been having such a good time living together and sharing the things we did that we just assumed writing would be one more thing to share." Though they have enjoyed great success in their partnership, they quickly learned that the collaborative process required much more of them than they had anticipated. They had to develop skills for resolving conflicts and differences of opinion that the writing brought out. They had to come to terms with each other's egos and idiosyncracies that they had been able to overlook until then.

Judith and her husband readily agree that working together makes extra demands on their marriage. Whereas going off to a job may be an escape from the relationship for many people, there is no such escape for the husband-wife team. They may be together twenty-four hours per day, for weeks on end, involved in the kind of creative activity that requires commitment and emotional involvement, bringing out both the best and the worst in each of them. Judith and Michael both believe that married couples, working together or not, need to have lives separate from each other. They make room for breaks by having lunch with a friend, or going shopping, or taking long, fast walks alone.

Both partners have their own outlets for tension—working off anger in hard physical work, athletic endeavors, or in hobbies that require great creative concentration. Judith cooks, sews, bakes bread, or refinishes a piece of furniture. Michael's stress reduction activities are more athletic in nature; he rides his exercise bicycle to work out his frustrations. In addition, he is an

avid photographer who spends hours taking pictures or printing in his darkroom. He finds it satisfying to have a creative activity that is completely his own.

Both Judith and Michael have learned that little peace offerings are important gestures that go a long way to renew bonds
and reduce tension. Such offerings need not be extravagant:
perhaps a gift from a shop passed during those long, fast walks.
This might be a piece of chocolate, or a card with a love note.

This writing couple agrees on five points that help them enjoy a successful partnership and harmonious marriage:

1. Have shared goals and agree upon strategies for achieving
   them.
2. Be open to compromise but don't lose your separate identi-
   ties.
3. Respect each other's talent and professionalism.
4. Be able to separate criticism of ideas from criticism of oneself.
5. Develop methods for preventing and reducing tension.

While Judith Michael sees these as guidelines for husband-
wife writing teams, the same points are undoubtedly good advice for any writing team, married or not.

It's not all hard work and struggle for Judith and Michael.
In fact, their enjoyment of each other's company has become an
integral part of their collaboration process. Describing how they
get their ideas for their books, Judith said, "We sit in the park or
walk by the lake and think about the dreams and fantasies and
hopes and fears that are shared by most people." This was the
source of their inspiration for *Deceptions,* which came out of Judith and Michael's realization that many people want to get away
from their own lives. It was the story of people who wanted to get
away, but at the same time wanted to keep their own lives, in case
they decided to go back to them.

Collaborators, whether they are husband-wife teams or just
business associates, have their own style of working. The Judith
Michael team has developed its own rules, beginning with talking out and writing a complete outline for the book, then having
long sessions, from a couple of days to a week, in which they
work over each chapter in detail. The detailed work on each

chapter includes talking about ideas, acting out dialogue, playing with the plot, and much note-taking. Eventually they come to an agreement on the action for the chapter, the characters involved, and how the characters will change or grow. Finally, they determine how one chapter will end so that it will lead into the one that will follow.

After the team is satisfied with a rough outline, Michael takes the notes and fine-tunes each chapter, scene by scene, to produce a detailed outline. Then Judith sits down at her word processor with these notes and begins writing the first draft.

As each chapter comes off the printer, Michael reads and critiques Judith's work. Judith describes this as "the opening gun for battle." The partners debate their ideas for anything from a few minutes to three days. Once their differences are resolved, by "intelligent compromise or total exhaustion," they put the draft of that chapter aside, with notes they have made along the way, and discuss the next chapter.

While Michael works on the detailed outline for the next chapter, Judith returns to the chapter they've just finished, and referring to the notes they've made, incorporates everything they've discussed and produces a second draft. This process is repeated about six times for each chapter. Judith says that by the time a chapter is finished, she and her husband's ideas are so interwoven that it is difficult to say "what belongs to either one of us."

SEPARATE VOICES, SEPARATE ROOMS

Husbands and wives often have their own writing careers separate from their collaborations. Such is the case with historians Oscar and Lilian Handlin. Oscar, a Harvard University historian, wrote *The Uprooted*, which earned him the Pulitzer Prize in History in 1951. Lilian's biography, *George Bancroft*, was published in 1984.

In an interview in *Publishers Weekly*, the interviewer said that the pleasure the Handlins took in their collaboration was quite obvious, and described their mutual respect as "palpable."

The Handlins work together in a small study on the top floor of the Widener Library at Harvard. They sit across the table from each other, surrounded by books stuffed with bookmarks and notes, to which they refer time and time again as they work. They talk to each other constantly, discussing the subject, taking notes, sharing references, philosophizing. In their work, they share the common theme which Oscar describes as "social history"—more specifically, what liberty means in the everyday lives of human beings through the ages.

Lilian Handlin insists that her husband is the senior member of the team as a historical authority. She says that she defers to his expertise whenever there is a controversy between them. However, Oscar sees their writing relationship as being much more a collaboration of equals. In a characteristically droll style, he describes the manner in which they work. He says: "She writes a draft of chapter two, I write a draft of chapter three, she tells me it's no good, I tell her it's no good."

THE IDEAL "COTTAGE INDUSTRY"

Mike and Nancy Samuels are a husband-wife writing team whose joint efforts have produced a half-dozen successful family health books. Mike was also Hal's first collaborator, the two of them having produced four books together, including *The Well Body Book*. Published in 1973, this book was instrumental in opening up the genre now called "self-help health."

Mike is a physician. His wife, Nancy, has a master's degree in education. Both of them are transplanted Easterners who moved to California in the 1960s, purchased a piece of land and took a year out to build their own home. Mike and Nancy are also parents, with two school-aged sons.

The Samuels' books include titles such as *The Well Pregnancy Book,* and *The Well Baby Book.* In a single room of the sprawling, rustic redwood home, which commands a spectacular view of the Pacific, the Samuels have a large desk with a computer on one end and a copy machine on the other. Most of their writing takes place here or in a business office set-up in what, from the exterior, appears to be a barn. Their computers serve two important functions for the Samuels: A word processor speeds up the tasks of writing, revising, and editing; a *modem* connects them electronically with data banks as far away as New York and Washington, D.C. By using their modem to connect them with medical centers doing research—the nearest one is fifty miles away—the Samuels save hundreds of hours every year that they would otherwise spend traveling to collect research.

After writing a half-dozen books together, the Samuels' work style is clearly defined. Mike does the medical research while Nancy crafts his notes—often scrawled out in the undecipherable shorthand that doctors are famous for—into sentences that people can read. Nancy also takes the role of patient-advocate, seeking answers to questions from the patient's perspective.

Although they talk through every piece of the book together, Mike is the organizer, the one who gathers the information together in a heap and, from his own notes, puts together a chapter outline from which to work. Nancy is the wordsmith, the one who writes and rewrites until the information Mike presents to her is in a form that is easy and entertaining for the nonmedical person to read. She is also the one who does the final editing of the finished manuscript, refining each sentence and sometimes restructuring a book before it goes off to the publisher.

Mike and Nancy frequently travel together on publicity tours and share the lecture podium when talking to groups about their books. Theirs is a perfect example of a profitable "cottage industry," allowing them to work at home. During a visit to the Samuels' home, one sees that family activity goes on in the midst of the writing, and the writing goes forward in spite of interruptions to drive to the next town to pick up one of their sons at a friend's house, or any one of an endless stream of tasks that keeps the family going.

The Samuels' collaboration has evolved over the years in much the way that marriages evolve, through give and take, trial and error, compromise, and ultimately a deeper understanding of each other. But in the final analysis, it is a division of labor, with a clear agreement about who is doing what, that keeps the team productive and the marriage vital.

TRIPLE THREATS

If you're thinking about a collaboration, don't overlook the possibility of working with more than one other person. There have been a number of successful writing teams in recent years that work this way. Justine Harlowe, as mentioned earlier, is the pseudonym for a writing team made up of three women: Jean Harvey, Tina MacKenzie and Laura Bennett. Together they produced the novel *Memory And Desire*. The story spanned three generations with scenes set in London, Rome, Venice, Paris, North Africa, the Caribbean, and the eastern United States. The wide variety of settings was possible because all three women had lived and worked around the world.

The three collaborators are the closest of friends. In addition to writing together, they often vacation together, in spite of having spouses and children who demand their attention. Laura Bennett, speaking for the trio, said: "We are all on the same wave length and are very much alike in many ways. We are all interested in people and situations and like to talk about them. What we have in common is that the book is our brainchild, separate from us, yet a growing, living thing that has to be tended to."

Laura Bennett—no relation to Hal—describes how the three women work together:

"Everyone bats ideas around while the person at the typewriter homogenizes the copy. We do a certain number of pages every day, then hash out how it will read and do a new copy. *Memory and Desire* had five drafts altogether. We edit simultaneously in one room and compromise on what to omit. The one at the typewriter records the flow of conversation, dialogue, and ideas and then we work with the rough draft afterwards. With three minds going so quickly, sometimes we have to use a tape recorder."

A similar but even more unusual collaboration is represented by the pseudonym "Monica Highland." The author of epic historical novels, Monica Highland is actually Lisa and Carolyn See, with a male ghostwriter, Carolyn's husband, making up the third "silent partner" of the team. What makes this team so unusual? Carolyn and Lisa are mother and daughter. Carolyn said of her first anxieties about writing with her daughter, "It was bad enough going shopping with Lisa and having my admittedly dubious taste questioned at every turn." With a curious grin she asks, "What if my subconscious turned out to be as tacky as my taste in clothes?"

Surprisingly, Carolyn and Lisa's collaboration brought them together in a way that probably no other activity could have. Working together, daring to share their "deepest, darkest secrets," they have learned to appreciate and respect each other—though as Carolyn admits, she's still not comfortable shopping for clothes with her daughter.

WORD BALLOONS

The writing team of Hal Blythe and Charlie Sweet goes by the name Hal Charles. Together the two men have written for most of the major mystery magazines, and created the Rex Rhodes, Kelly Locke, and Josh Holliday mystery series.

Hal and Charlie state that their individual egos dissolved long ago, replaced by a single voice to which they both contribute in their writing. This voice, known as Hal Charles, has written: "Over the years our collaboration has become so much of a natural process that we're rarely conscious of individual contributions—each remark is an unattributed word balloon."

Like the authors of *Auntie Mame* and *Inherit The Wind,* Blythe and Sweet are attracted to team writing for what might broadly be described as social reasons. Hal Charles says, "Collaborating is a lot of fun. It gives us a chance to socialize, to share common concerns from local traffic patterns to the international heroin traffic." They share the belief that team-writing is one of the best forms of insurance against burnout, since one or the other of the writers is always ready with a fresh idea to spur the other on.

For them, the entire composing process is a team effort, with both men taking part from the beginning of a project and staying with it to the end. They set up specific times to work together. They say that, "From the first sentence to the final word on the final draft, everything is a collective effort."

To begin a project, they brainstorm together. For example,

an idea for one story they wrote grew out of their common interest in the work of Edgar Allan Poe and their both having grown up with games like Clue and Scrabble. The phrase "a dying clue" came out of one of their brainstorming sessions—who thought of it first, neither can recall—and from that they found it easy to visualize a dying person, the victim of a murder, placing three letters on a Scrabble rack: POE. That image became the basis for their story.

As a novel or short story unfolds, Charlie takes the role of the scribe, putting the words down on paper and rewriting as they go along. Hal pays more attention to the direction of each paragraph as well as the overall piece. As Hal Charles tells it, "You might say one of us functions as the right brain while the other works as the left. Our advantage is that we can both use both sides at once."

The Hal Charles team plays out many of the scenes they write, before committing them to paper. Blythe and Sweet describe how they often carry this role-playing activity into restaurants and other public places. More than once people in neighboring restaurant booths have mistaken them for cops, as they discussed their latest "case," or graphically described the discovery of their latest victim. Indeed, as writers they imagine themselves as all the characters in their stories. And just as a detective might do, talking shop over lunch comes naturally—regardless of how disconcerting or intriguing such a conversation might be to the people who overhear them.

Even marketing and sending out query letters is a joint effort for them. Hal types cover letters while Charlie runs off the manuscripts on the printer. These writers claim that their greatest creation hasn't been Rex Rhodes, Kelly Locke, or Josh Holliday, the lead characters of their series, but Hal Charles himself. They say that because of this creation, "writing is not an agonizing and lonely profession" for them.

WRITING IN ABSENTIA

Not all collaborations work like the ones above. Hal Bennett has been involved with three collaborations in which there was minimal contact between himself and his coauthors. In one case, a publisher hired him to rewrite the book of a particularly vain author. The author had insisted that no one but the editor and himself be allowed to see the manuscript before its publication. The editor assigned to the book, however, had neither the writing skills nor the time required to whip the book into shape.

Hal had worked with this editor in the past, and after several meetings they reached an agreement. Hal would rewrite the author's material and communicate directly with the editor. The editor would get credit for the work and the author would not be told that anyone else had worked on it. Part of the agreement was that Hal would never let it be known that he had done the writing.

As it turned out, the author was more than satisfied with the writing his "editor" had done, leading to a volatile situation because that author submitted the rough draft for a second book which the same editor wanted to publish. The problem was that Hal had other commitments and could not work on this second book. In the end, the editor had to reject the book, not wanting to risk the chance of the author discovering what had occurred.

Probably one of the most unusual collaborations Hal was involved with was his coauthorship with John Marino, the organizer and originator of RAAM ("Ride Across America"), the transcontinental bicycle race staged every year. Now covered by "ABC Wide World of Sports" and other media, the ride attracts racers from all over the world.

John Marino is a colorful character who has twice held the world's record for this ride. The story of how this came about was one of the things that attracted Hal to this writing partnership in the first place. Right out of college, John was drafted by the Los Angeles Dodgers, but in training camp he fractured two vertebrae. Doctors told him that although he would recover from this injury, he could never play baseball again, and would have to limit strenuous activity.

John endured a great deal of pain for months following the injury and, despondent about never being able to play sports again, he allowed his health to decline. He got worse and worse, finally "hitting bottom." Then he began a long quest to regain his health and considered getting back into sports.

After nearly two years on a strict regimen, John discovered that he could ride a bicycle with relative comfort and that he had great stamina. One afternoon, he was looking through the *Guinness Book of World Records* and noticed that the record for the ride across America had not been challenged in nearly ten years. He decided to set a new world's record.

John trained vigorously, and in the summer of 1976, was ready for the challenge. On that first try, he bettered the last record by three days and eleven hours. In 1981, he rode again, this time breaking his own record by twenty-one hours.

Hal met John Marino and proposed a collaboration while John was in training for his second record-breaking ride. The publisher of the as-yet-unwritten book, Jeremy Tarcher, wanted the book's publication to coincide with the end of John's race, since television coverage would provide free nationwide promotion. The problem was that John—an ex-English teacher—couldn't both write his book and train for the race.

Hal went to Los Angeles, met with John, and was given a huge box of papers that contained the research and first draft of the book. While Hal sorted through this material in the weeks ahead, John trained. There were frequent phone calls back and forth as the writing got under way. When the day came that John was to begin his big ride, a support crew had been assembled to escort him across the country, a film crew was in place, and the publisher had assembled all the pieces to rush the manuscript through production, in order to have finished books available as soon after the race as possible. Hal and John were, however, still working on the final manuscript.

So it was that while John Marino was making his 1981 record-breaking ride across America, he was also writing his book. During his breaks, John telephoned Hal, sometimes thousands of miles away, to approve final revisions and help fill in dates, names, and ideas for the final pages of the book. Hal recalls getting calls from John at roadside telephone booths in the heat of the Arizona desert and in the midst of driving rains in Kansas and Nebraska, with John's voice always filled with energy and enthusiasm, as though riding across the United States to set a new world's record was a pleasant and exciting but nevertheless common occurrence.

On other occasions, Hal has written with lecturers whose busy schedules took them far from home. One such book, *Peak Performance: Lessons From The World's Greatest Athletes,* was written with Charles Garfield, one of the world's foremost authorities on mental training in sports. Much of this book was written through phone calls and correspondence between the two authors. At one point, three edited chapters were lost in the mail, somewhere between Idaho, where Charles was lecturing at the time, and California, where Hal was writing, when the secretarial service Charles hired to do mailing for him mailed the work to the wrong address.

Although the error was finally corrected, with the edited materials chasing Charles around the country on his busy lecture schedule for nearly two weeks, the loss of the edited work caused both writers anxious moments.

For Hal, there is no best way to work with a collaborator. Each new collaboration will be slightly different, in part because the key players are different, in part because the subject is different, and in part because you have learned something about collaborating, from the previous project, that will make the next one easier. Our advice is to learn everything you possibly can learn about collaborative writing—the pitfalls as well as the pleasures. Learn all you can about putting together productive collaborations, and then tailor your knowledge to fit your particular situation. Use the material we present here as your basic resource. Then let your own judgment and creativity be your guide in using it.

5

NINE EASY PIECES—
THE FOUNDATION
FOR SUCCESS

Many years ago, Hal's writing teacher and mentor, award-winning novelist Wright Morris, said: "To write well, begin with an idea that impassions you. Without that you are simply going through a mechanical process, and you might as well be pumping gas at the filling station." Although that advice was given to a group of budding young novelists and poets, it is just as true if you are exploring collaboration. Before examining why this is true, let's take a look at nine key steps that will help you launch your collaborative writing project. These will provide the guidelines for getting the most from this chapter:

NINE EASY PIECES FOR SUCCESSFUL COLLABORATION

1. Find an idea that you feel passionate about.

2. Research and develop your idea so that it can be presented to collaborator/experts, agents, and editors in a coherent and interesting way. An important part of this work is to explore the market for your book: why people will want to buy your book; what competing books are on the market; why your book is different and better than others.

3. Seek out a collaborator. Do this by "positioning" yourself where you are most likely to connect with the right person to fill your bill—and be ready to present your idea to whomever you meet. Go to professional association meetings where you are most likely to meet experts in your area of interest, or if you're working on a novel, join a writer's organization group (attend classes, conferences, etc.), or contact a literary agent who might connect you with a collaborator.

4. Develop a working agreement with your collaborator. Put *everything* you can in writing.

5. Work with your collaborator to develop your idea and write a proposal. If you are working on a novel, write sample chapters.

6. Submit your proposal to agents or publishers. If you are working on a first novel or book of short stories, most agents and editors will want to see the finished work, although they will want to start with a sample chapter and a synopsis.

7. Write the book.

8. Promote the book (as the writer, you may or may not be involved in this aspect of the project).

9. Optional: Start working on the next book with your collaborator.

GOLDEN IDEAS, GOLDEN OPPORTUNITIES

Hal's first collaborative writing project, a medical book for people with no medical training, was one that completely captured his attention. He lived it and breathed it for five years after his prolonged stay in the hospital, where he saw the need for such a book through the eyes of patients who were frightened and in pain. Firsthand experience and a sense of mission kept him going, even though agents, editors, and publishers told him there was little chance of selling the book without having the proper credentials.

The medical book eventually materialized, not because Hal went out and got a medical education, but because he kept his

eyes and ears open until he found a person with medi
tials who shared his beliefs and who was interested in co...
ing on a book with him.

The lesson here is that if you have a dream that grabs you, hold on to it regardless of the present problems you might perceive. Eventually, you will find a way to get your idea into a published book.

Put yourself in the offensive position; that is, see yourself as the prime mover of a project. You are the person looking for someone who can work with you in the development of your idea. Although it *can* be done, you are in a weaker negotiating position if you go out hitch-hiking, that is, presenting yourself as a writer looking for a person with an idea who might take you along for the ride.

You could argue that William Novak wasn't impassioned by the idea for writing a book with Lee Iacocca. At least Novak wasn't the one who initiated the idea. However, he had written three books of his own and had established himself as a business writer. His agent also recognized that Novak could collaborate with a man like Iacocca.

OBJECTIVE OBSERVERS AND IDEA GENERATORS

In the old school of journalism, writers were supposed to be objective observers who recorded exactly what they saw. The good journalist was like a camera in this respect, "documenting" rather than "interpreting." Hunter Thompson's and Tom Wolfe's brands of journalism changed all that. They showed that the objective eye was a myth.

From an agent's or publisher's point of view, the objective eye school of journalism usually is not a strong position for a collaborator to take, although it does fit the mold for the old style ghostwriter, who invested little of him or her self in the project.

It is often surprising to discover how many writers there are out there who, like publishers, are searching for people with a project, book idea, concept, story, or theme that will capture the imagination, love, and devotion of the book-buying public. One of our favorite *New Yorker* cartoons shows two women nursing cocktails, with one saying to the other: "I'm marrying Marvin. I think there's a book in it." What's needed is not more writers looking for people with ideas that they might hook up with, but more writers who can generate ideas of their own, and who can also collaborate with other writers or experts. In *The Craft of Writing,* William Sloane remarks: "There are no uninteresting subjects, only uninteresting writers."

Before you do anything, find your idea. Immerse yourself in that idea. Eat it, drink it, and sleep it. If the idea warrants it, dedicate the next month or the next year or even the rest of your life to it. Then, if it's something that can best be done with a collaborator/expert, start putting out feelers for that person. How do you do that? It may be much easier than you think.

Are you having difficulty finding salable book ideas? If so, the following list can help you. Read it over and pay particular attention to those subjects that spark your interest and imagination. If anything will, those are the subjects that will make you an interesting writer.

SUBJECT LIST

Sex	Science
Love	Technology
Adventure	Social progress
People overcoming obstacles	The family
Mysteries	International intrigue
Self-improvement	Inspirational writing
Humorous situations	A hobby or personal interest
Spirituality	Crime
Business	Money
Politics	The rich and famous
Use and abuse of power	Good triumphing over evil

Exposés	Travels to exotic settings
The arts	Biographies
History	Family sagas
The future	The rise of heroic figures
Health and wellness	Ethnicity
Warfare and revolution	Socioeconomics

Identify your own interests, and trust them to guide you in choosing a subject to write about; your interest in the subject will come through in everything you write, and that is what will attract an editor's, and then the reader's attention. Make lists of your favorite books, beginning with the first one you can remember, and make brief notes on what you liked about each one. This exercise will help you focus on what inspires you to write, because you will enjoy writing what you most enjoy reading. Your passion will inspire your best writing. And your best writing will inspire the best efforts to sell your manuscript.

And don't forget your own experience when you're looking for an inspiring writing project. J.P. Donleavy once said: "Writing is turning one's worst moments into money." In a similar vein, Philip Roth said: "Nothing bad can happen to a writer. Everything is material."

Make a list of your most important moments, both good and bad. Make notes to yourself as you play with the possibility of how each experience from your past might be shaped into characters, scenes, or ideas for books.

What subjects have you already written about? What are the areas of your own expertise?

Keep in mind that two or more years may elapse between the time that you first get your idea and the time the book is written, sold, and published. Ask yourself: What will the world be like in two years? What will people want to read about then? You probably don't own a crystal ball to accurately predict the future, but pretend that you do anyway. What will interest you, for example, in the areas of sex, politics, business, science, relationships, health, crime, money? Read *Megatrends* for a glimpse into the directions our society is taking us. Put yourself in a publisher or editor's shoes, wondering where to invest your publishing dollars. See if your guesses don't lead you to the subject for a book.

Like your ability to write, your ideas are your stock in trade. Get into the habit of keeping a notebook or cassette recorder handy so that you can make notes on them whenever you wish.

Hal rarely goes anywhere in his car without taking along a miniature cassette recorder. Some of his best ideas have either come to him or have been developed while stuck in traffic on the freeways. When traveling on airplanes he is never without a notebook or his briefcase-sized, battery-operated electronic typewriter. Once, while flying between San Francisco and New York, he had a breakthrough with a book idea he'd been working on. He was surrounded by distractions. There was a movie showing in the cabin, and the couple in the seat behind him was having a bitter argument. To escape all this, Hal took his tape recorder, locked himself in the lavatory and dictated notes for forty-five minutes, until the stewardess came knocking on the door to find out what had happened to him.

Many writers get their best ideas between 11 P.M. and 8 A.M., while most sane people are sound asleep. To take advantage of this time, keep a tape recorder or a notebook at your bedside and get into the habit of using those creative moments.

Keep a file of your notes. If you're using a tape recorder, jot down titles or brief descriptions to identify what's on each tape so that you can find them in the future. Sooner or later you will find a use for anything that comes to mind and that you feel is worth recording.

LINKING IDEAS WITH COLLABORATORS

Let's say you want to write a popular book on building individual retirement funds, and you know nothing about the subject yourself. How would you go about finding an expert to work with you? The easiest, most direct way is to go to the Chamber of

Commerce and ask for lists of professional associations in the
area of your interest.

Most professional associations have regular monthly meetings that are open to nonmembers. You pick out a couple of
promising associations, make a few calls to find out when the
next meeting is scheduled, and then start attending. Some professional associations don't allow nonmembers into their meetings unless they are sponsored by a member. To solve this problem, talk with the contact person that the association lists with the
Chamber of Commerce. Tell him or her what you're doing and
why you wish to attend their meetings. Nine times out of ten that
contact person will sponsor you, and may even introduce you to
people who can help you. By doing this, you've put yourself
right into the middle of the experts you're looking for, and you'll
find someone who shares your views and wants to write a book
with you.

Tom Mease, a Los Angeles-based writer, had an idea for
developing a how-to book to help people who wanted to get
started in the import business. He called the Chamber of Commerce and was given a list of associations for people with import-
export shops and mail-order businesses throughout the county.
On one of the lists he recognized the name of an old college
roommate. He contacted this person, they had lunch together,
and out of that meeting they developed an idea for a book that
they would self-publish and market by direct mail. The book
sold for $10 a copy, and three years later they had sold over
150,000 copies!

Of course, there are books whose central ideas won't be
aided by such a plan. Let's say, for example, that you have an
idea for a novel. You're not a fiction writer—up to now your
main interest has been writing self-improvement articles for a
women's magazine—but you are a good story teller and you have
put together the outline for a novel based on the life of a contro-
versial public figure. You've researched your subject, using news
clippings, excerpts from radio and television interviews with the
person, and you've figured out a way to disguise the character in
your novel so that you are not putting yourself in a position that
will attract a libel suit. You've put all of this into a proposal and
yet you still feel that you need a collaborator who can render an

exciting scene and write believable dialogue—two things that you either can't do or don't want to do.

Recognize that at this point you have a salable package. You aren't any longer a writer looking for a project to hook into; you're a writer with a solid project of your own, and you're looking for someone who can provide you with a needed service. You are in the driver's seat. You're not out hitchhiking for a ride.

The next step—if you have a proposal or manuscript—is to go to a literary agent. When you do this, put yourself in the position of being an entrepreneur seeking a partner with skills or resources to help you carry out your plan. You are going to the literary agent for two reasons: first, to find out if your idea really is salable, and second, to find a collaborator who will be turned on by the idea, who can write well, and whose "chemistry" promises to mix with your own. Beyond that, look for a person with an established track record, someone who has written and published a book with a major publisher or perhaps has published a story or two with a reputable magazine.

If your idea is good, and your book outline looks professional, a literary agent may very well be interested in helping put together your team. Knowing writers is an agent's bread and butter, and with the growing popularity of collaborative writing, agents are more than ever looking for the ingredients for successful writing teams.

Although literary agents are logical resources for finding collaborators, never overlook your friends and close associates as possible coauthors. The story of Justine Harlowe (Jean Harvey, Tina MacKenzie and Laura Bennett) is an object lesson here. For years this trio had taken vacations together and had never discussed each other's writing aspirations. Then, on one of the vacation trips, they were discussing their summer reading lists and decided that they could "do better than the books we saw out there." Partly in jest, the three friends began concocting a story about a character they called Natasha de Vernay. The idea caught on for them. Natasha became the protagonist for their novel *Memory And Desire,* which established the friends as a writing team.

As a collaborative writer, take the initiative. And if you have an idea that you are convinced is good—regardless of what anyone else says, stick with it. The power of that kind of passion is phenomenal. Just keep building on what turns you on and eventually, believe it or not, you will get what you're looking for. Dreams really do come true in this business, but sometimes one has to keep polishing the dream until it sparkles like a diamond.

FROM ARTICLE TO BOOK

Very often the expert you are looking for is right under your nose. Where, then, is he or she hiding? The answer may be between the covers of your favorite magazine or professional journal.

Look for articles that are related to your topic. The author of such an article may turn out to be your expert collaborator. Why, you ask, would a person who knows how to write team up with another writer? First of all, don't jump to the conclusion that an expert whose name appears as the author of an article really knows how to write. The editorial staff may have burned the midnight oil to hammer the expert's ideas into a publishable form. They may have worked from lecture notes, lab notes, taped interviews, or a hastily put together draft by the expert and his or her secretary. The expert may, moreover, have gotten enough of a taste of what it could be to be a writer that he or she will be both flattered and intrigued to be approached as a collaborator.

Similarly, people who write magazine articles can't necessarily write books—and vice versa. Hal has worked as a consultant and ghost for a number of writers whose primary skills and interests were in writing for magazines and professional journals. As such, they had a knack for putting together short, succinct pieces but had great difficulty shifting to a longer form. Such collaborations are often excellent because both parties have a common interest and sensitivity as writers.

LOOKING FOR WRITERS

If you are an expert looking for a writer who will collaborate with you, many of the same suggestions will apply for you as will apply for finding a ghost with more limited responsibilities. You might like to go back to Chapter 3 to review some of the suggestions we made there, or to look over the list of organizations for making contact with writers.

THE LUCK FACTOR

It is interesting to note that when asked for their tips on how to break into collaborative writing, some of the most successful collaborators shrug their shoulders and say it was "pure luck." But probing a little deeper, we found that all of those asked were driven by a dream, the idea or the vision for a book that excited them. And they stuck with the dream, believing in it even when others didn't. There was a very successful West Coast publisher who, upon retiring from the business, was asked what characterized the most successful writers he'd published. He said, "They were all very stubborn people when it came to their own ideas. Their success was 10 percent talent and 90 percent tenacity."

Jim Cash, the film writer we discussed in the previous chapter, describes the chance meeting when Jack Epps enrolled in his script-writing class at Michigan State. But how much of that meeting really was pure luck? Prior to their meeting, Jim had spent two years tape-recording dialogue from old movies and then transcribing it, word for word, to study movie dialogue styles. He was so passionate about the dream of writing film scripts that even this arduous and seemingly unrewarding task—one that would have driven most writers crazy—came easily for him.

By the time he met Jack Epps, Cash already had a large personal investment in his art. He was determined to become a successful film writer and unconsciously he was always on the lookout for opportunities that would help him realize that dream. This attracted him to people with similar goals, people like Jack, who had enrolled in Cash's script-writing class because he had already made the decision to go to Hollywood and become a script writer. All these associations may seem like "luck" to the key players but to an outsider looking in, the collaboration came about because the authors were highly motivated. Luck is ability meeting opportunity.

PITFALLS TO AVOID

We won't dwell long on this subject, but there are situations to avoid as a collaborative writer. For example, there's the "everyone-has-a-wonderful-story-to-tell" syndrome. You've probably been in situations at parties or on the commuter bus when, upon mentioning that you are a writer, somebody offers to let you in on "the story of the century." The following happened to Hal:

"The name's Tom Johnson," the party guest said, shaking Hal's hand and simultaneously pulling him away from the other guests. Tom was in his late fifties, visiting from Cincinnati, was a good sixty pounds overweight, and wore an impeccably tailored, double-breasted, gray pinstripe suit. He held a cigarette in the same hand that he held his drink, though he never once put either to his lips. His tenor voice somehow didn't match his physical appearance or his aggressive manner. Hyperventilating, he stopped every two or three sentences to catch his breath, with an asthmatic wheeze.

"So you're a writer! You know, people are always telling me I should write a book. But I don't have your talents to shape the story into words, you know what I mean. It takes a very special person like yourself to do that. I've always had a great deal of admiration for people who can write."

Hal confesses to feeling flattered by Tom's estimation of his abilities so he stands by, ready to soak up whatever Tom is willing to hand out in the way of compliments. That he didn't know Hal's name, much less what he had written, until a few moments ago, didn't daunt him. After all, like most writers, Hal has learned to accept praise from any source.

"I've had a fascinating life, just fascinating," Tom says. "I've lived all over the world, been everyplace."

"I see," Hal says.

"The stories I can tell you! One time my wife and I were down in Brazil on a business trip, and we happened to be dining at the Hotel Ritz when who should walk in and take the table right next to ours but Lucille Ball and her husband, you know, the Cuban bandleader, what's-his-name?"

"Desi Arnaz," Hal says.

"That's him, yes." Tom says this with a great sense of finality, as though he has just said something profound.

Hal keeps silent, waiting for the story to unfold. Tom keeps silent, waiting for Hal's response. The silence builds until finally Tom is forced to speak.

He says, "Another time we were over in France, staying at some fancy place the tour group had booked for us. We'd been everywhere in Europe, seen everything. This was our second trip over there in five years. Well, I was having lunch with my wife and I got the idea that we should just sort of strike out on our own and really meet the people of France on their own terms."

Tom's voice drones on as he narrates a story of walking around Paris "unescorted" in the middle of the afternoon. Minor event after minor event occurs, with little or nothing to distinguish one from another. And now the picture becomes clear to Hal. Tom is so thoroughly self-involved that he is unable to see that the little events that excite him hold no interest for anyone else.

Hal finds an excuse to escape from Tom. He is beginning to understand why people have advised Tom to write a book. A book you can close and put away on the shelf. Hal does escape, but not before he has been shamed into exchanging business cards with Tom and discovering only too late that Tom is going to telephone him to discuss collaborating on a book. Tom, of course, is certain his life story will make a best-seller.

Although the Tom Johnson story is an extreme case, the lesson is clear. Hal and Michael frequently come across people who, although not themselves writers, are certain they have fascinating stories to tell, or who have ideas the world is just dying to hear.

There are thousands of Tom Johnsons out there, and there are also people like the ninety-year-old grandmother who telephoned Hal from Indiana at least once a month for nearly a year, trying to persuade him to write her book for her. She had a "sure preventative" for the common cold that consisted of gargling with ginger tea every morning. "I've done it for the past thirty years," she said, "and I haven't had a cold in all that time." She was certain that single idea could be "made into a book that would bring millions of people wonderful comfort." And because Hal had once written a book on colds and flu, which the grandmother from Indiana had borrowed from the library, she was certain he was the right person for the job.

PROTECT YOUR TIME AND ENERGY

If you have ambitions as a collaborative writer, be aware that by announcing your profession you are opening yourself up to everyone who is convinced that his or her life story or pet idea or theory about how to save the world is material for a best-seller. As a collaborative writer, you are this person's godsend, the answer to dreams and prayers. All you have to do is write down what that person has to say and you'll both get rich and famous.

The truth is that probably most people do, as the old saying goes, have a book *in them*—and most of the time that is the best place for it. The real work in writing any book, collaboration or not, is researching that material and putting it into a form that will capture the interest and the imagination first of an editor and then of the reading public.

As a collaborative writer, you want people to know what you do. Nothing in publishing is more powerful than word-of-mouth advertising. But making that information public opens you up to the Tom Johnsons and the Indiana grandmothers with cold cures. Much of the time, people who approach writers with book ideas are not as off-the-wall as the examples given. But these examples point out the necessity for creating a filter for protecting yourself so that you don't waste your talent and your energy on projects that will never get further than the proposal stage. How do you create such a filter? You do it by keeping at least part of your attention focused on the hard realities of the business end of writing.

Publishing a book represents a major investment. In a crowded, competitive marketplace, a book will usually be offered to the reading public with little or no advertising. Unless the story or the idea has solid potential for grabbing the reader's interest, the investment in the book—yours as well as the publisher's—will be wasted.

Before getting involved in a collaborative project, ask yourself the following: Who is the reader you wish to reach? Who will buy the book? What purpose will the book serve in people's lives? Ultimately, a book's success in the marketplace will be dependent on whether or not it meets a need for a great many people.

This is not to say that there aren't great works of poetry or fiction that have only a limited market. Some of the greatest works of art haven't enjoyed popularity during the artist's lifetime. Melville's *Moby Dick* was a commercial failure in his lifetime, gaining only a handful of loyal readers. It was not recognized as a classic until after he died.

SCOUTING THE LECTURE CIRCUIT

There are four good reasons that writers as well as agents, editors, and publishers scout the lecture circuits for collaborators. Although we have briefly discussed these in previous pages, it is worth exploring them in greater detail.

First, professional lecturers are highly visible, usually traveling from city to city, appearing in panel discussions, and doing radio, television, magazine, and newspaper interviews. That high visibility means that their names are recognized by a large number of people and name recognition sells books.

Second, a lecturer's career is greatly enhanced by the publication of a book, and lecturers who know their business also know this. This means that if you were to approach a lecturer with a book idea, most would be more than open to at least sitting down and talking with you.

Third, since lecturers are public people, you have the opportunity to get to know a little about who they are without putting yourself on the line. All you risk is the cost of tickets to get in to hear their lectures. Although the person you see on the podium is not necessarily the same personality you will have to work with—successful lecturers are also gifted actors—you will at least be able to get a sense of who the person is and whether or not your chemistry and his or hers will blend.

Fourth, lecturers are communicators, and so you and they have compatible interests. This is not always true of other experts. But be warned: Lecturers and writers speak two different languages. One would think that it would be natural for lecturers to also be writers, but this frequently is not the case. Lecturing and writing are two very different forms of communication. To get just a hint of why this is so, try to recall the last time you heard someone try to read a book to an audience. Although there are exceptions, even some of the best fiction begins to sound slow, ponderously detailed, and just plain boring when read aloud. Lecturers must deliver their whole message in an hour or less, while a book may take days or even months. Many excellent lecturers simply don't have the patience for writing a book—assuming they even have the time, which is usually not the case. That's why they need writers like you.

Gordon Burgett is a writer and publisher who travels and teaches seminars through the California state college circuit. He teaches classes on writing, book publishing, cassette tape publishing, and giving seminars. A number of years ago, Burgett teamed up with Mike Frank, a professional speaker who, unlike Burgett, is well-known in speaking circles. The result was a book on public speaking by a public speaking expert, written by an expert writer. Since both men were on the lecture circuit, they had a ready market for it and their subsequent books, making them available to everyone attending their courses.

As a writer, you are offering a much-needed service to the lecturer. Some, of course, already have writers working for them. You can easily find this information by looking at *Books In Print* and finding out if the lecturers you're interested in have published books under their own names. If they have several books in print, chances are their book-writing needs are already taken care of. But if you find a particular lecturer you would really love to collaborate with, don't assume that he doesn't need you. He might just have severed relationships with his old writer. Or she might have decided she simply can't keep doing her own writing—and thus they are wide open to your help. Or, if you have a good book idea in mind, they might jump at the idea of collaborating with you.

Where do you get the names of professional lecturers? The most obvious and accessible source of names and schedules is the Sunday entertainment supplement of your newspaper. Popular lecturers depend on these announcements.

Lecturers who specialize in business also place ads in trade magazines and newspapers. Such ads not only give schedules but usually describe the material being covered. "Name" and entertainment lecturers may be listed in entertainment magazines like *Variety*.

In addition to the professional lecturer who may give an hour-long speech and then be on to the next town, there is the lecturer whose main product is a one- or two-day workshop or seminar. Such workshops may be on anything from making millions in real estate to raising one's self-esteem or learning how to cope with teenaged children.

Such workshops are particularly adaptable to book form, since they are usually well organized and divided into manageable parts that can easily translate to the chapters of a how-to or self-improvement book.

Many, if not most, workshop directors give free one-hour lectures to introduce what they will be doing in the workshop itself. These are frequently delivered at hotels or other public places that can draw foot traffic as well as accommodate people who see the announcement of the lecture in the local newspaper. These free lectures also provide you, the collaborative writer, with an opportunity to see what that person is doing and to introduce yourself.

Most lecturers make themselves available to the public either during a break or after the lecture. Use this opportunity to introduce yourself and ask if it would be possible for you to contact the lecturer in the next day or two to discuss a book idea. If it is true, introduce yourself as a professional writer with good contacts in the publishing world. If that's not true, at least be able to present a business card and a brief description of the book project you have in mind. (If you don't have a business card and stationery, get thee to a printer and have them made this week. They'll do wonders to establish your professional image.)

Still another source of experts—and one often overlooked—is the professional cooking teacher. Cookbooks, like diet books, are consistent sellers. If you're a writer who also loves to cook, you probably are aware of the culinary circuit, or "food mafia," as insiders call it. There is a whole subculture of people who take cooking classes and attend demonstrations with super-stars like Julia Child and Alice Waters. The cooking classes and demonstrations are publicized through culinary stores (that's kitchen supply stores to the uninitiated). Again, the same things that apply to other lecturers apply to cooking instructors; they want books to help promote their classes and they usually don't have time to write them.

Several years ago, a friend of Hal's contacted him to ask about book contracts. She said she was in the middle of talks with a publisher on a cookbook. Hal answered a few of her questions and then asked her what the project was. She replied that it was "sort of a collaboration." With whom, Hal wanted to know. "Well," replied his friend, "I really can't say until the contract is signed." Two months later, with contract in hand, his friend explained what she had meant when she described the project as "sort of a collaboration." The collaborator was "Fannie Farmer," a character based on a real person but developed by the publisher for the cookbook series by that name. Hal's friend's name, Marion Cunningham, would win wide recognition as the person who resurrected Fannie's name in *The New Fannie Farmer Cookbook*.

Does the idea of offering lecturers your services as a writer contradict the theme with which we began this chapter—that you should begin with an idea you are passionate about? Absolutely not. Even though the expert you're going to may have an established subject area, he or she may not have considered all the ways that subject area can be presented in a book. For example, the Thai cooking instructor may never have considered the idea of writing a book, complete with full-color photos, called *Thai Appetizers for That Special Party*. Similarly, the person who gives workshops on making a million in real estate may never have considered applying the same principles to the American family buying a home, which you feel will make a highly salable book.

Don't approach a lecturer blindly. Start with a sense of what kinds of books readers will want in two years, and what subjects you want to write about. Develop an idea. And then seek out the lecturer or lecturers who might fit in with your plans.

SOURCES FOR LECTURES AND WORKSHOPS

In addition to the above general suggestions for making contact with lecturers and workshop directors, the following sources offer catalogs and course descriptions that will not only narrow the field for you but may also help you generate book ideas.

Colleges and Universities

Most universities and community colleges have guest lecture programs that are open to the public, either free or for a small fee. Continuing education departments also offer classes— sometimes weekend seminars, sometimes spreading over several weeks—by experts in their fields. Catalogs give names, dates, times, and class descriptions that may help you generate ideas.

Continuing Education in Industry

Many companies have training offices that sponsor seminars and classes for their employees. Any association you have with such companies can become a resource for you. Perhaps your mate or a friend works for a company with a training office that can supply you with schedules or even brochures from companies offering seminars. You may also get information of this kind from trade journals that are usually available at training offices.

Mantread, Inc.

Mantread is a nonprofit clearing house on information about training programs, workshops, and lecturers, especially those directed to the business community. It publishes a National Training Registry, which reports on the experiences of people who have participated in such programs. You must be a Mantread subscriber to get this information but if you have a friend in a company training office, that person usually has access to Mantread's National Training Registry. You can get more information directly from Mantread, whose address is 46 East 4th Street, Saint Paul, Minnesota 55101.

Seminar Catalogs

There are a number of national associations that provide information and catalogs on seminars. These specialize in workshops and training programs aimed at the business community. They are:

American Management Association
135 W. 50th St.
New York, NY 10020

AMR International, Inc.
1370 Ave. of the Americas
New York, NY 10019

New York Management Center, Inc.
360 Lexington Ave.
New York, NY 10017

GOOD SPORTS AND INTERESTING ORGANIZATIONS

Any person or organization that has high visibility is a prospect for a successful book collaboration. Two excellent examples are professional athletes whom the media consider "newsworthy," and clubs with large memberships or newsworthy missions.

Several years ago, a young man by the name of Dan Poynter got the idea for doing a book on the popular Frisbee. He was a marketing genius, coming up with the idea of packaging a handbook with a Frisbee, making it an item that could sell in bookstores, toy stores, sporting-goods stores, and swim gear boutiques—since Frisbees are associated with the beach. Although he knew how to package, produce, and distribute the book, Poynter was not an expert at the game itself.

Poynter teamed up with Frisbee champion Mark Danna. The latter wrote the how-to chapters of the book, with Poynter filling in on history, competition, and record attempts. He also assembled the appendix. The finished package was the phenomenally successful *Frisbee Players' Handbook*.

A number of years ago, the Girls Club of Santa Barbara was

in financial crisis. A woman by the name of Mindy Bingham, an idea person and organizer, turned the club around and made it a financial success, with a book. Mindy got the idea for a book for teenage girls on personal planning and self-awareness. She roughed out the ideas for the book, incorporating question- naires and exercises. She then worked with collaborator Judy Edmondson, who researched and developed more tests and ex- ercises. Then the whole manuscript was sent to Sandy Stryker, an advertising copywriter, who rewrote the manuscript, adding continuity and stylistic "punch." That book could never have gotten into print had it not been for this three-woman writing team.

WRITING WITH FRIENDS

There was an article by a prestigious New York literary agent— who shall remain unnamed—that appeared in a publishing magazine. It glibly stated: "If you are considering a writing col- laboration with a friend, stop right now. Sooner or later you will be forced to make a choice between the business of writing a book and the pleasure of that friendship. You might as well make that choice right away, rather than be forced into it under duress, a month or two down the line."

Although collaborations admittedly put pressures on friendships, we don't agree with the distinguished agent's ad- vice. Some of the publishing world's most successful collabora- tions have been between friends, the one between Stephen King and Peter Straub on *The Talisman* being one prime example. Hal has worked on a number of collaborations with people who quickly became friends as the projects progressed. Some of the relationships that he has established through his writing have become some of the most important friendships in his life.

However, the agent's glib advice has a purpose—to remind us that collaborations make demands that go quite beyond the business of filling pages with words or working out a plot. There are egos involved, and the business of writing a book with anoth- er person is an intimate one.

Successful collaborators agree on two points in working with someone close: First, the collaborators must have strong mutual respect for each other's talent or expertise; second, the writing collaboration should be based on the fact that you share an idea about which you both feel passionate. In the latter respect, the "mission" of writing the book, not the friendship, should be the central motive for the collaboration.

This brings us to the subject of the next chapter—People Skills—and the realization that without such skills, no matter what your abilities as a writer, you will not complete your collaborative project. You don't need to be a psychologist to make a collaboration work well, but you do need humility, the ability to compromise, and managerial skills.

6

PEOPLE SKILLS—THE KEYS OF PRODUCTIVITY

Agatha Christie once said: "I've always believed in writing without a collaborator, because where two people are writing the same book, each believes he gets all the worries and only half the royalties." Jim Comiskey, a business consultant and the author of *How to Start, Expand, and Sell A Business,* offered this advice to his readers: "Be very cautious about partnerships. They seem to be so easy to get into and so difficult to get out of."

Why start this chapter on a negative note? The answer is that collaboration is not always easy. During the course of writing and publishing a book, you can be sure that problems, tiny and large, will arise. And yet, the rewards of collaboration can be so great that we believe developing the expertise to make it work well is a worthwhile mission. Just as there are those who advise against marriage, there are those who advise against collaboration. But of both collaboration and marriage we might say that their success or failure is not inherent in the institutions themselves but in one's preparation for them. With this in mind, we echo the words of Shakespeare, "Hasty marriages seldom proveth well."

The lessons we offer here, and for that matter throughout the book, are intended to expand your skills and insights into putting together a productive and rewarding collaboration.

The following information provides you with a preview of the issues we'll cover in this chapter. After reading this chapter, these points will serve as a reminder of the key issues to keep in mind in the formative stages of a collaboration.

THE TEN ELEMENTS FOR SUCCESS

Look for the following ten elements in any collaborative arrangement you're considering. It is a good idea to review this list before your first meeting.

1. Credentials, contacts, specific skills, writing experience, expertise: Does the person have credentials or a license in his or her field of expertise? Has the writer been published? Is the person able to deliver on the concrete things you are seeking from him or her? Who will provide or be responsible for whatever research interviews or other resources you'll need?

2. Promotion: What kind of a promotion campaign for the book can you and your collaborator put into the proposal to help sell it to a publisher?

3. Differences: Is the person different from you, with a different outlook on life, and thus able to bring a dimension to the project that you would not have alone?

4. Mutual Respect: Is the person as interested in you and your perspectives as you are in him and his perspectives?

5. Commitment: How committed is this person to completing the project?

6. Flexibility: Is this person willing to compromise, allowing that your ideas, although different from his or hers, are also valid?

7. Management Awareness: Does this person have or recognize the need for management skills to keep the project going smoothly?

8. Rules of the Road: Do you and your collaborator agree on issues such as editorial control, money, division of work, how the authors' credit will read, and getting a "divorce" if the collaboration doesn't work out?

9. Gut Feelings: How comfortable do you feel being in the same room with your collaborator? Can you look each other in the eyes?

10. Planning: Who will do the planning for the project, outlining the material, researching, collecting resources, working out timetables?

GETTING DOWN TO BUSINESS

Be prepared to judge the merits of a collaborator in one or two meetings. But on what basis will you do this? What will you be looking for? Are there particular questions to ask? What kind of information should you be willing to give your possible collaborator about yourself so that he or she can make a judgment about working with you?

PREPARING FOR THE INTERVIEW

The easiest place to start any interview is with objective information such as credentials, when this is relevant to the project you're developing. Depending on your motives for seeking a collaborator, credentials may be extremely important—as in the case of writing a scientific or medical book—or they may be relatively insignificant—as in the case of writing a novel. For example, if I were seeking a collaborator who could be an aggressive promoter for the book, I'd want to know about his or her experience talking with large groups, doing television and radio interviews, and generating the kind of visibility I want for the book.

If I were seeking a collaborator who was an expert in a particular field, I'd want to see evidence of that expertise. This evidence might be in the form of university degrees, in papers published in scholarly or professional journals, or in simply having an established name in the field. If the collaboration involved a medical or scientific subject, I'd want to make certain that the collaborator had formal credentials, such as a Ph.D., an M.D., an R.N., or a similar degree or state license to put on the cover of the book to help establish credibility with agents and editors and, later, in the marketplace.

Sometimes the credentials you'll be looking for will be less concrete than college degrees or licenses. For example, if you were seeking a collaboration with a person who had an inside track on a famous person or an important news story, you'd want to make certain that this person can really deliver. You'd want to ask questions relating directly to the information or "inside track" you wished to have, and the answers would have to be specific and dead on target. Look for information the person has right now—not information he or she will be able to get if such-and-such happens. Don't tie yourself into any collaboration based on "ifs."

Credentials for a novelist are more difficult to judge. Obviously, if the person is an established writer, with one or two books in print, you have a body of material on which to base your judgment. Read the material and see how you like it. If the person is not published, ask to see samples of his work, or ask him to write a chapter with you. Look for the writing skills you want. For example, if you need someone who can write lively dialogue, look for that. If you need someone who can render exciting action scenes, look for that. If you're seeking a writer who knows how to develop plot or characters, look for samples of that kind of work.

Make yourself a checklist of the kinds of things you want from the person you are to meet. Make sure you know why you're seeking this particular collaborator—and then make certain he or she can deliver. Go to the meetings prepared, but don't go with a checklist of questions in your hand so that the person feels like you're taking a deposition. That is not only rude, it's unprofessional.

The best interviews flow smoothly and naturally. You're not there to interrogate or to be interrogated. Why not? Because if the collaboration is to be successful, the association you will establish will be an intimate one, one that will stretch out over several months, or up to a couple of years, and it is a good idea to establish the quality you'd like in that relationship from the moment you meet. Never lose sight of the fact that you're probably going to be spending a lot of time with this person, and you will want to conduct every phase of your business together—from the first interview on—with that in mind. Don't do anything in the initial interview that might later be a bone of contention. Conduct yourself as though you were being introduced to someone with whom you are going to establish a long-term, friendly, and productive working relationship. Always act as if everything you do will succeed. Confidence is contagious.

This brings us to the less concrete part of the interview, that of trying to define the human qualities to look for in a potential collaborator. The best way to do this is to explore the experiences of established collaborators, writers who know what goes into a successful coauthorship.

LOOKING FOR MR. OR MS. GOODWORD

Science fiction writer Michael A. Banks described human qualities that went into being a good collaborator: "The ideal collaborator is a writer who is flexible, can take criticism, overcome his or her own ego, and work on a regular basis." This is a tall order, of course, but tracing the experiences of collaborative writers gives us direct guidance in achieving the collaborators' "state of grace" that Banks describes.

The ideal collaboration, most publishing people agree, is a 50-50 proposition. On the most obvious level, that means the collaborators share income equally. But something even more important than that occurs on a deeper level; call it respect, call it mutual admiration, call it an awareness of the value of each other's contribution to the book. After all, in many collaborations, the subject couldn't get a book written without the writer and the writer wouldn't have a story to tell without the subject. This kind of balance, a sense that your partner is making a contribution equal to yours, and that he or she feels the same way about you, is not always easy to come by. Where do you begin building this kind of mutual respect?

The answer is much simpler than you might suspect: Begin your collaboration looking for the differences between you and your potential writing partner, rather than the similarities. As contradictory as this may sound, it is out of the differences that the true power and excitement of your collaboration will evolve. Your acknowledgment of and appreciation for the differences will ultimately create a third voice (or ego) described by successful collaborators—which is unlike either of your own.

Hal Charles (collaborators Hal Blythe and Charlie Sweet) said that their collaborative process become so natural to them that they rarely are conscious of "individual contributions." A similar sense of working together as a perfectly matched team has been reported by collaborative writers who have written together a number of years. This kind of team effort, born out of mutual respect, probably evolves through collaborating on a number of projects, the way mutual respect and love evolve through trial and error in a healthy marriage.

Ego is perhaps the biggest struggle in any collaboration. Authors, like other creative people, must have a certain confidence or even stubbornness about their *inner self*, which includes that part of them commonly called the ego. The ego, after all, is the container for so much of the material or thinking that goes into a book. Conflicts arise in collaborations, not because these wonderful inner resources are available, but because the person who possesses them believes that only he is right or that somehow he's been granted the exclusive copyright on truth.

Twenty years ago, Hal once had an opportunity to coauthor a book with a person who was a widely known lecturer on alternative education. This man, whom we will call Dr. Star for reasons that will become clear in a moment, invited Hal to his home in San Francisco. The interview took place in the living room, which was cluttered with his children's toys. In the adjacent kitchen, Dr. Star's harried wife prepared dinner for six guests who were due shortly. The couple's two unruly children, ages four and six, ran around the house shrieking and playing noisily, demanding but not getting their father's, Hal's, and their mother's attention. The noise level in the house increased as the children escalated their efforts and their father, oblivious to it all, talked louder and faster in an effort to tell Hal about the project.

Dr. Star paced up and down the living room, gesticulating wildly as he told story after story about his own exploits as a famous person. He talked about being on the Johnny Carson show, how he had lunch with Phil Donahue, how he had shared a podium with the noted psychoanalyst Karen Horney when he was still a graduate student at Harvard. One story blurred into another, with children literally pulling at his pantlegs and screaming. At one point his now half-hysterical wife stuck her head out of the kitchen long enough to remind him that the children should go to the baby sitter's soon, and he should get himself ready, and she would like some help with last-minute preparations, and did he remember that he had to pick up bread and a cake she'd ordered from the bakery, before it closed? Dr. Star answered these cries for help with annoyance, insisting that he was quite capable of assuming these responsibilities but that he had business to transact with Hal.

Hal made efforts to discuss the project and Dr. Star said not to worry. It would be a wonderful book, he said, and he assured Hal that he already had the outline "all worked out in my head."

Hal had just published a successful book of his own on alternative education, based on his own experiences as a teacher and program director, and he had many things he wished to share with Dr. Star, perhaps putting them into the book they might write together. However, in the hour he spent with this man, there was not a single opportunity to discuss Hal's ideas. It was obvious that Dr. Star required center stage at all times, not only when he was at the podium but in his own living room, and even with his own wife and children.

The collaboration went no further than this interview, since it revealed to Hal that an association with this person would only mean becoming an audience and scribe for Dr. Star. There could have been little room for anything but the great man's ego.

Although an extreme case, this story does provide guidelines for recognizing the kind of coauthor who will not be interested in you and your contribution to the project—unless you can act as an extension of that person. If you're looking for a working relationship based on mutual respect, one in which your input is as important as the other person's, Dr. Star is a model for the sort of person to avoid.

Although there are exceptions, many stars and celebrities are assertive, self-important people, and those same qualities that might make you feel unimportant in their presence may contribute much to their charisma on stage or in the public eye. In the proper context, such personality traits come off as self-confidence and can be tremendously charismatic for large audiences. As a theater director friend of ours once said of the performer's ego, "It comes off a lot different on the stage than it does in your kitchen over burnt toast and yesterday's warmed-up coffee."

If you are interested in a collaboration with a "star," be prepared to put that person first. After all, if the book you wish to write is about that person, it will be your responsibility to keep the spotlight focused anyway. Be willing to serve, to confine your contribution to the writing and shaping of the book.

Unless doing a book with a star is your goal, what would be an example of an open collaboration?

WHEN DIFFERENCE BECOMES STRENGTH

Sometimes a "magic," a "personal chemistry" draws collaborators together and carries them along without a hitch. But in most cases that kind of personal chemistry is the product, not of magic, but of just plain people skill, the ability to let another person into your life and to enjoy that person, not because he or she is exactly like you but because you are different.

Jerome Lawrence has a broad view of the ego, a philosophical perspective that undoubtedly contributes to his harmonious association with Robert E. Lee. Both men appear to enjoy the other's ego, to value it as much as they value their own, and to recognize the wealth of experience both egos can provide in writing a play. Lawrence has said that a large part of the reason for their success as a team is not that they are alike, or that they have similar egos, or that they see things in parallel, but that they "are very different." Agreeing on this point, Lee says, "Jerry's viewpoint is often considerably at odds with mine," but this is seldom a source of trouble so much as a source of rich contrast, a way of seeing something more than either man could see if he were working alone. It is *synergy* in action, an example of how 1 + 1 can equal 3.

A COLLABORATOR'S CHECKLIST OF DO'S AND DON'TS

Don't	Do
Jump into a collaboration without getting to know your coauthor.	Get to know your collaborator through a series of get-acquainted meetings.
Sign onto a project that either doesn't interest you or that offends you.	Commit yourself only to projects about which you feel passionate.
Start writing before you define your working relationship.	Use a "Stepped Agreement" (pages 92-93) to minimize risk; define the work in writing.
Assume that the other person's research is complete.	Make certain you see all research, interviews, or other materials required to write the manuscript.
Make changes on the manuscript without consulting your coauthor.	Discuss all changes with your collaborator—preferably in writing.
Have surreptitious meetings with your editor.	Make certain your collaborator knows everything that you know.
Lock horns with your collaborator.	Seek out the help of a third party (your agent, editor, etc.) to assist in settling disputes.
Go too long without meetings to discuss the progress of the book.	Schedule regular work meetings to compare notes, share concerns and ideas, and read each other's material.

Lee expands on this notion, saying, "I remember something one way, Jerry recalls it another. . . . It is simply the parallax of personalities." Lawrence calls this "creative memory," explaining: "You have an obligation to be creative with personal memory and with history. Facts change depending on which part of the elephant you touch."

The lesson in this is that collaborations begin to click, begin to develop their own magic, when the writing partners stop looking for total agreement, or stop looking for proof that their own way of seeing is better than their partner's, or stop looking for a mirror likeness of themselves in the other person, and start looking upon the differences as a way of expanding their writing resources. This is the essence of a truly inspired collaboration, which creates a new and extraordinary reality out of the combined efforts of two rather ordinary egos.

Novelists Virginia Watson-Rouslin and Jean M. Peck said about their collaboration: "One benefit (of collaborating) is the wider range of experience and knowledge that two contributors can bring to a writing project. Don't, therefore, be put off if a potential collaborator's interests and yours are antithetical. These differences are your strengths." How are they strengths? Watson-Rouslin and Peck say that they bring you into "different social circles" and that in doing so, "you're coming into contact with different people and extra sources for story ideas."

MOVING FORWARD

Assuming that you agree with these collaborators' views of the ego, how do you maintain such a perspective throughout the year or more that it may take to write your book? To do so, keep your attention focused on the book project itself. Remind yourself constantly that writing your book is your mission, a mission that you share with your partner. If the accomplishment of that mission is compelling to you both—and it should be—it will help you transcend those inevitable conflicts that will arise wherever two or more people are working together. Sometimes it isn't easy to remember that a book is a project, a thing, a physical entity, and that creating it is not unlike creating any other thing, be it a loaf of bread, a flower garden, a house, or a giant corporation.

In larger projects, the necessity for cooperation and good management is obvious; one person can't do it all, nor can the larger vision be achieved without the cooperation of all concerned. But when writing a book is approached with the businesslike perspective of a corporate planner or a contractor building a house, the mission of building that thing, and the necessity of seeing that many egos will be involved in its construction, force us to move from an attitude of self-centeredness and selfishness into a position of management and cooperation.

PATIENCE, MY DEAR WATSON!

Editors who specialize in working on collaborative writing projects can judge and comment on the pros and cons, the joys and problems of collaboration. Nessa Rapaport, senior editor at Bantam Books, has worked on a number of successful projects, including Lee Iacocca's biography, Geraldine Ferraro's biography, and President Carter's memoirs. We asked her what she felt was the single most important piece of advice she might offer collaborators. She replied, unequivocally: "It always takes much longer than you think it will."

On the surface this advice may seem obvious, but it may be obvious only to an experienced writer. It may not be obvious to the nonwriter who is the other half of your writing team. On Hal's first collaboration with Mike Samuels, the medical half of *The Well Body Book*, Mike became very impatient with how long it was taking to finish the book. His impatience became a source of tension in their work, at times impeding progress. As it was, Hal and Mike finished that first book in just under nine months, a near record for a 500-page manuscript that often required the authors to translate highly technical medical information into language that the general reader will enjoy reading.

Years and several books later, Mike apologized to Hal for his impatience with that first project. He confessed that his expectations had been entirely unrealistic. He had believed that he would sit down with Hal, spend a few hours "talking the material into a tape recorder," and then Hal would take the tapes home and turn them into a book.

At the time Hal and Mike worked together on that project, Hal had several published books to his credit, though up to then none of them had been written collaboratively. As a seasoned author, it didn't even occur to him that another person might not understand that you didn't write a book overnight.

How long should it take to write a book? That, of course, depends on a number of variables:

- How long the book is
- The kind of material involved (translating technical data into everyday language takes longer)
- How much research, permissions, and illustration work needs to be done
- How well the collaborators work together
- How much "creative brainstorming" is required
- Whether or not the collaborators can devote full time to writing

If all goes relatively smoothly, most experienced collaborative writers calculate that fifteen to twenty manuscript pages per week is a respectable average. That's figuring three to four months to write a 250-page manuscript. There are, of course, weeks when you will produce two or three times that many pages, but there are also weeks when you won't be adding to the page count because you are editing or rewriting already completed chapters.

Unless your collaborator is working beside you, he or she won't be able to see what you are doing, or why you aren't getting on with it.

It's important for the nonwriter to understand that much of the craft of writing is invisible. A professional writer knows that a sentence that might look fine in a letter to a friend, or even in a business report, can become a glaring embarrassment when committed to cold type on the printed page. Honing sentences, shaping paragraphs, rearranging the order in which the material is presented in a book, are all skills that make a writer a professional. What he or she does to accomplish those things often seems like nit-picking, compulsive behavior, or even out-and-out obstructionism to the nonwriter. Few nonwriters know the hidden truth in the words of Richard Brinsley Sheridan:

"You write with ease to show your breeding,
But easy writing's curst hard reading."

Nor do they know what must be done to make "easy writing" into easy reading—that four or five drafts of "difficult writing" may be required along the way.

What do you do to educate your nonwriting collaborator so that he may appreciate the time you're putting into the book? Let him or her know about this issue before you sign a contract or writing agreement. Give him this book to read, and make certain that you highlight this section with a yellow ink marker.

MANAGING FOR SUCCESS

Wherever more than one person is involved, the success or failure of the association will depend, in large measure, on at least one person in the project having or being able to develop management skills. What does this mean? It means that the first priority is the completion of the book. To do that, of course, one has to acknowledge the egos and the special needs of the individuals involved and to look for ways that those needs can best be directed into the fulfillment of the central mission.

When you get to the point of realizing that this management perspective is necessary, take a look at basic business management books. You don't need to study management in depth, but you do need managerial detachment, the perspective that to make things work well between people you should know how to step outside your own ego, relying on managerial techniques rather than your own feelings. *The One Minute Manager,* a book that established itself as a classic in management technique in the first year of its publication, is a good place to start, if only because it can be read from cover to cover in about an hour.

Another book that will be helpful is Robert Bramson's *Coping With Difficult People.* Both *One Minute Manager* and *Coping* are easy reading. Bramson's book, in fact, can be used like a reference for picking up general guidelines for managing difficult personality types. This book can be scanned in an hour or less, so that you will know enough about what it offers in the way of managerial tips so that, should you need it, you can turn back to it for more advice. Ask your collaborator to read these books too.

WARNING SIGNS

If any of the six following warning signs occur, take it as a signal that there is a need for a change in your relationship. There are relatively simple solutions to most problems, such as making up assignment lists to clarify responsibilities. But there are times when you will have to confront your collaborator and make your complaints known.

If everything you do fails to bring about satisfactory changes, you may need to seek the aid of your agent or—if you have a close working relationship—your editor.

A third party mediator may also be necessary if conflicts continue and your agent or editor can't help. This might be a mutual friend, an attorney who is skilled in mediation, a marriage and family counselor, or a business consultant who practices mediation.

Continued violations, in spite of all you do, means that it is time to dissolve this collaboration and seek a more productive one.

1. Undelivered Goods

The Sign	What It Could Mean
Difficulty getting your collaborator to deliver on promised research or other materials	The materials may not exist, or may not be in that person's possession, regardless of what you have been told.

What To Do

Make an "Assignment Sheet" (see the following example) of the material you need. Sit down with your collaborator and get a commitment on dates he or she will deliver the materials to you. Each of you should keep a copy of this list. As each promised delivery date arrives, make certain the promise has been fulfilled. In most cases, you will discover that systematic record keeping of this kind will solve the problem, although you may continue to have to be the one who handles such logistics, keeping track of dates and who does what. If the collaborator still isn't accountable for assignments, you will have to confront him or her directly. The collaborator may wish to hire a third person to complete such work.

Assignment Sheet					
Date Noted	Work to Do	By Whom?	Target Date to Complete	Date Com-pleted	Comments
			(Use full sheet horizontal 8½″ × 14″)		

2. No Show, No Go

The Sign	*What It Could Mean*
Collaborator doesn't return phone calls or fails to respond to your letters.	Collaborator has lost interest or is not living up to his or her part of the agreement.

What To Do

Set up a standing time and day for progress reports, preferably on at least a weekly basis. Example: "Let's check in with each other by phone (or in person) every Friday between 11:00 and 11:30 A.M." Then, both of you need to honor that, calling to make your progress report and check in with the other person, even if it is to say that you have nothing to discuss at this time.

3. Nobody Minding the Store

The Sign	*What It Could Mean*
Collaborator fails to incorporate changes or ideas you have suggested.	Collaborator is not taking notes during meetings with you, is deliberately ignoring you, or simply has trouble with logistics.

What To Do

Set up an "Editorial Sheet" (see next page). Use it for noting any editorial changes you or your collaborator wish to make. Always make a copy for yourself as well as your partner. Communicate all editorial comments in this way. Fill in all blanks as each step is completed. This keeps both collaborators accountable on all editorial changes, minimizing controversy and error.

Editorial Sheet			
Location Page & Paragraph	Editorial Comment	Who will make change in ms.	Date Completed
	(Use full sheet horizontal 8½″ × 14″)		

4. Copy Cat

The Sign	*What It Could Mean*
Collaborator is duplicating your work.	Collaborator is unclear about who should be doing what.

What To Do

Set up an "Assignment Sheet" (see page 79).

5. The Star Syndrome

The Sign	*What It Could Mean*
Collaborator dominates all meetings, giving you little or no time to discuss your ideas.	Collaborator wants full control of the book and does not wish to incorporate your ideas.

What To Do

If you are working with a person who is an expert or a public figure, and the book is mainly about that person or his or her work, you may have to give up your desire to contribute more actively to the book. On the other hand, if your agreement is that you are equals, you need to be clearer about setting limits. The simplest way to do this is through using the assignment sheet. However, if you are continuously feeling pushed aside, you need to be direct about communicating this to the other person. Do it in writing, stating clearly one or two situations where this has happened, and clearly stating how you would like to be heard. Many people are unaware of stepping on other people's toes in this way, and are willing to make changes. But they need to hear the problem from you.

6. Emotional Pile Ups

The Sign	What It Could Mean
You find it difficult to be in the same room with your collaborator.	You are resentful or angry and are not expressing what's bothering you.

What To Do

Sit down alone and make a list of the things that bother you about your collaborator. Remind yourself that this list is for you and you alone. You need not show it to the other person. List small things that may have annoyed you—like never cleaning his or her coffee cup after an editorial meeting at your office—as well as the big things—hands you all his editorial notes in a childish scrawl that takes hours to decipher. Then choose two or three issues (no more) that you would like to have solved right now.

Have a meeting with your collaborator and put these things on the line, with constructive suggestions for solutions. Example: "It annoys me that you always leave your coffee cup around after our meetings. I'd like you to rinse it out and leave it in the kitchen sink before you leave." Or, "I can't decipher your handwritten notes. Could you please type them out for me, or print them in a way I can read?"

When problems and grievances get stored up too long, there is often a tendency to really unload when you do open up. You may unload so much at one time that the other person feels completely overwhelmed and hopeless about ever being able to satisfy what he or she perceives as "demands." To guard against this happening, limit yourself to three complaints (less, if possible). Write down what you want and discipline yourself to sticking to that course of action. Rein yourself in if you feel yourself deviating from the agenda. Both of you should read these warning signs and encourage each other to bring up problems before they become serious.

THE IMPORTANCE OF BEING PRODUCTIVE

Collaborating author Janet Gluckman observes, "How you split up the work has to do, in largest measure, with who does what best." If, for example, you love research and your potential partner dislikes it, find that out before you start working. Tell your collaborator the kinds of things you like to do best, and find out what his strengths are. Discuss how to work together so that both your preferences are honored and used. You can complement each other's strengths and weaknesses.

In their collaborative work on four books, Hal and his coauthor Michael Samuels sat down in the same room and worked out each step of the project point by point. They developed the book concepts and the detailed working outlines together. Then they divided up the initial research, that is, reading for the project, with Hal taking the more popular books and Mike, being the medical person, taking the technical journals and computer data banks. They met once each week and went over their findings, incorporating what they had found into their working outline. Finally, they sat down with their books and other research materials spread out around them, and began writing. They produced the rough drafts together, with Hal keying in the material, sometimes in shorthand form, on the word processor, while Mike pulled references from books. There were always surprises as they worked, with new thoughts being triggered as they went along. With the work style they developed, there was room to change the outline—or the whole direction of the book—if new ideas generated along the way warranted it.

Many collaborators structure their work relationships around productivity. Jerome Lawrence and Robert Lee's goal, for example, is to work six days a week and produce five pages every day. They work face to face, much as Hal and Mike Samuels did, although they may also work over the phone, using headsets to keep their hands free at the word processor. In most cases, they contribute equally to build a scene or develop a character.

By contrast, other collaborators divide the book up into segments, usually chapters, with each writer taking half the chapters to work on alone, then later coming together to integrate their separate work.

For this book, Michael and Hal wrote a proposal together. That is, without a doubt, the best way to get to know a collaborator. Michael and Hal discussed the material in face-to-face meetings, and with phone calls, with Hal doing writing and Michael doing research on contracts, gathering articles about collaborative writing, sharing stories and experiences of the business from an agent-author's point of view. As the proposal and then the manuscript itself were produced, Hal sent the written work off to Michael for his editorial comments, followed up by meetings to discuss improvements and additions.

All of the above are just models, not prescriptions, for the ways collaborative writers can work together. Let the models give you the raw material for discussing different work styles you can develop with your coauthor. Use the first couple of meetings together to kick around the possibilities. Something different from the models we describe above may evolve.

EXPLORE YOUR EXPECTATIONS

New York lawyer Mark L. Levine, whose specialty is negotiating book contracts, for writers and small publishers, says: "Collaborating—especially on a book—can be dangerous, unless you and your coauthor first agree, in writing, about your financial arrangements." And here's where money becomes a people skill.

Before you put a single word of the book down on paper, discuss your separate expectations about how you will divide up the writing responsibilities and divide the income from the project. At a seminar for "Writers Connection" in California, publishing attorney and author Brad Bunnin outlined four chief areas of concern for collaborators. These are:

1. Control
2. Income
3. Splitting of work
4. What to do if one of the coauthors wants a divorce

These four points are discussed in the following chapter on

contracts. But it is important, even before you get into writing contracts, to explore these points in an informal way.

1. *Control.* This covers a big territory. For example, who will have final say in editorial judgments such as word selection, length of scenes, the inclusion of sexual content in a novel or short story, and the length of the book. A good way to broach these subjects with your coauthor is to open a discussion by recounting experiences you have had in the past.

For example, "In my last collaboration, with Tom Goforitt, he blocked out the scenes for each chapter. Then we sat down and discussed each one, point by point, with me making suggestions for any changes I saw. Would an arrangement like that be comfortable for you?" If you have not previously collaborated, you might say the same thing but from one step removed: "I recently read that it is a good idea for one person to block out the scenes for each chapter and then sit down with the other person and discuss any changes or improvements they might make. That makes sense to me. How does it seem to you?"

2. *Income.* How you handle Bunnin's second point, income, will depend on whether or not you have an agent. If you do have an agent, your money discussions should be with him or her rather than with your coauthor. Then leave any negotiations up to your agent; don't discuss money with your coauthor. However, if you don't yet have an agent for your project, open discussions about money frankly and honestly. If you would like your share of the income to be 50 percent, say so. Find out where you both stand on money as soon as you can.

3. *Splitting the Work.* Sit down alone and figure out how you would like to divide up the work. Then take that information to your coauthor. You might say, for example, "I'd like to talk with you about how we might divide the work. I've sketched out one plan that I would be comfortable with. I wonder if you could take a look at it and discuss how this would work for you."

4. *Getting a Divorce.* It is important to recognize that painful or unproductive collaborations stretch out for months, and sometimes years, not because the parties involved really choose to continue but because they don't know how to get out of the situation. You would be amazed at how much pressure is avoided in collaborations by discussing this point at the outset. Present the issue to your collaborator in an open, and possibly light manner. After you've read the next chapter you'll know what the issues are. The main issue is, "If we have to get a divorce, who gets custody of the proposal or manuscript we've developed together?"

For some reason, most writers are uncomfortable talking about these things—perhaps because we are, at heart, hopeless romantics who prefer to think that money is not important where a good cause is involved. Or, perhaps it has something to do with the fear of rejection; we don't want to put these issues on the line for fear of offending the other person. But if you express such concerns and your discussions cause offense, they have also served a valuable function, revealing that your collaborator isn't someone you can work with. Collaborators must be able to talk openly with each other—at least about mutual business matters—and should be able to agree on basic points. If they can't, chances are they won't be able to agree on emotional and procedural issues during the day-to-day process of writing.

Look upon everything we've discussed in this chapter as being a way for you to get to know your collaborator. Even more than getting questions answered, and beginning to define a working relationship, you'll be testing the waters, trying out the chemistry for your team.

DETAILS! DETAILS!

For some people details such as whether or not they will get bylines are minor issues. For others they are crucial indeed. Whose name will appear on the book? Whose name will go first? In the case of a celebrity collaboration, should the writer's name appear at all? Some writers are content with being anonymous, as long as the royalties keep rolling in, while others want their names boldly splashed over the cover. These are details that you should introduce in the first meetings with your collaborator.

Other details to discuss: Who will agent the book? Who will

do the publicity tour? If there is a separate property involved in the book, such as a training program that you have developed on your own, does your coauthor understand that the program will continue to be your property? Are there audio or video cassette programs involved, and if so who will have the rights to them? Does the material you're developing have a market as a film—feature film or television miniseries? Is there a possibility that your agent can sell foreign rights?

Where will the authors meet when they work together? Will Hal go to Mike's place or vice versa, and if one person is doing all the traveling, will he or she be reimbursed for his travels by the other person? Create an expense fund and agree that any expense over $50 must be approved by both coauthors.

Who pays for lunches?

How do you keep an accounting of telephone calls? What about typists' fees? Will transcriptions be made? If so, who pays?

Will you work with computers? And if so, how? Are your computers compatible so that you can exchange disks and transfer files? Can you work a modem hookup, or is that not worth the effort? Are your writing programs compatible?

What times of the day do you each do your best work? This may seem like a small thing but think what a struggle it could become if the time your partner wants to get together with you turns out to be your lowest ebb of the day, the time when you usually curl up on your couch for a nap?

Quirks and nuances of character do affect collaborations. Because each individual is different, it's impossible to anticipate every issue that might arise in the course of these first meetings. But the bottom line will be much simpler than any of the things we've discussed: How do you feel being with this person? Be honest with yourself about this. Trust your instincts.

During your meetings, do you feel that you are having trouble being heard, or do you feel that there is an easy exchange between you and the other person? After your meetings, do you feel exhausted and depressed or stimulated and energetic? Do you find yourself tightening up certain muscles in your body when you are together—your buttocks, back, shoulder, or jaw muscles? Or do you feel relaxed and at ease, loose and open? If you feel nervous or overwhelmed because this person is a celebrity, are these feelings going to get in your way as you write, or do you enjoy the prospect of helping in the development of the book?

Above all, be honest with yourself and straightforward with your collaborator. Remember that getting to know the other person is as important for him or her as it is for you. Be generous about giving information about yourself. This generosity will more than pay off as the two of you are drawn together as a writing team.

Having passed the initial interviews with flying colors, you are ready to map out the details of your collaboration and put specifics down on paper. The following chapter describes how to do this so that your agreement is well-defined and your roles clearly stated.

7

AGREEMENTS AND CONTRACTS—DEFINING WORKING RELATIONSHIPS

You've found someone you feel will be a compatible writing partner. You've had a meeting or two to size each other up. You feel good about your budding collaboration, and you're onto an idea that promises to produce, if not a best-seller, at least a publishable book that will be personally satisfying and financially rewarding for you both. All you have to do is sit down and start writing.

We wish we could tell you it was going to be that easy. However, there's another important step you must take if you want everything to go smoothly—and that has to do with contracts.

GOOD CONTRACTS MAKE GOOD COLLABORATORS

Robert Frost disapproved of the notion that "Good fences make good neighbors," but the clear definition of boundaries and ties between you and your collaborator can mean the difference between a bitter feud and a friendly, productive relationship. With apologies to the poet, we believe that "Good contracts make good collaborators."

Although there may be other subjects more exciting and romantic, it is often the contract that makes the difference between a partnership fraught with problems and one that goes smoothly, leaving plenty of room for both the romance of being a writer and writing the book.

THREE FORMS OF CONTRACTS

Before you start writing, familiarize yourself with three basic kinds of contracts: Collaborators' Contracts; Agents' Contracts; and Publishers' Contracts:

• *Collaborators' Contracts:* This is a contract between you and your writing partner. It defines your responsibilities prior to the sale of the book to a publisher. Such a contract may be prepared as a "Statement of Intent," written in letter form. (See pages 99-100.)

• *Agents' Contracts:* This refers to the contract, or contracts, that you and your collaborator have with a literary agent—or agents, if you and your collaborator have different ones. (See Appendix D.)

• *Publishers' Contracts:* This, of course, is the big contract toward which all your efforts will be directed—the contract with a publisher who wants to produce your book. (See Appendix E.)

STEPPED AGREEMENT: THE PAPER THAT KEEPS THE CREATIVE FIRES BURNING

Before you're ready for the formal "marriage" of a contract, you and your collaborator need to move through the stages of getting to know each other, specifying who does what, and developing your joint project from an idea to a definite plan.

The initial weeks of a new collaboration are like the opening of a new love affair. In the first flush of excitement, everything seems possible, because nothing has been put to the test. It is all dream, all fantasy and speculation, in which you see what you want to see. There is an aura of self-assurance and goodwill, and in light of these good feelings, it may be difficult to imagine that there might be hard times in store.

To avoid hard times, we have this one piece of advice to offer you: "Get to know each other very, very well before you make the long-term commitment of signing a contract to do a book together." Consider what might happen if you discover, after investing money—yours or your publisher's—and months of your time, that you and your collaborator just aren't compatible? You've come to an impasse and there's nothing to do but cut and run. This situation doesn't happen *often,* but it does happen *sometimes,* and one excellent way to avoid such a calamity is to follow what we call the "Stepped Agreement."

The Stepped Agreement is not a contract. It's a five-step process, with each step an agreement between collaborators to complete a specified amount of work. Each step is based on knowledge you've gleaned from the previous step, and the risk is minimal each step of the way.

In courtship the goal in such a process is to establish a relationship that can last. With collaborative writing, the goal of the Stepped Agreement process is to establish whether or not you want to sign a Collaborators' Contract with your associate. Each step in the process takes you closer to a contract—or makes it clear to you that you should terminate the relationship.

Between the two of us (Michael and Hal) we have been involved with more than fifty collaborations. These have ranged from collaborations between people who were total strangers before they took on their writing partnerships, to husband and wife teams who presumably knew each other about as well as anyone has a right to expect. The compensations involved have ranged from flat fees for ghosting, to advances against royalties, to combinations of these two. Looking back over these collaborations, it is not easy to make many sweeping generalizations about them—except that even when you think you know a person well, you may be in for unpleasant surprises unless you sit down and take the time to define your working relationship from the very beginning.

STEPPED AGREEMENTS: THE PROCESS SIMPLIFIED

Note that these five steps are written from the writer's point of view. If you are the expert working with a writer, you will be the one who initiates these steps, and you should transpose the material accordingly.

Step One: Look Over the Materials
Make an agreement, clearly stated either orally or in writing, that you will look over materials your collaborator has collected or produced for the book. State how much time you will spend doing this, and whether or not you wish to be paid for your work.

Step Two: Write a Letter of Response
After looking over the above, write a letter containing: (1) your feedback on the material, such as overall impressions, whether or not the material interests you, and whether or not you feel there is sufficient material for a book; (2) a short, rough description of the book you imagine growing out of this material. Include in this description a list of books already in print, which cover a similar subject, and might be compared to the book you would like to write together, a description of the targeted reader (general reader, professional, educational market, etc.) you imagine; and (3) a closing line pointing the way ahead, inviting your collaborator to work with you on developing a more comprehensive outline for the book.

Step Three: The Rough Outline
Working together, you and your collaborator produce a rough working outline for the book, based on your discussions and any material your collaborator has supplied. Plan on writing between ten and twenty pages together, outlining the contents of the book chapter by chapter. (Details of what such an outline contains are given later in this chapter.)

Step Four: The Agreement to Write a Proposal
A book proposal can be seventy-five pages in length or more, with sample chapters and all the other elements that go into it. You could easily invest six weeks of your time in this. Both you and

your collaborator should understand this, and if you are expecting payment for this work you should put that in writing. Write a letter describing what this proposal will contain (more about this later), how much time it will take, and how much input you will expect from your collaborator. If you wish to be paid for this work, tell your collaborator how much.

Step Five: Write a Collaboration Agreement
Having succeeded in all of the above, you will now go on to contract with your collaborator to write your book together.

===

Why is such a process advisable? Our experience with collaboration has taught us that a specific, written statement can save hours of frustration and disappointment. Consider the following.

HIGH HORSES ON HIGH TOWERS

Several years ago, Hal met with a potential collaborator who had been referred to him by mutual friends. Arthur Hightower (not his real name) was an anthropology professor at the same university where Hal had completed his undergraduate work. Their first two meetings went well and both men were excited about the prospect of doing a book together. Dr. Hightower had an idea for a book based on a paper he'd recently published in a professional journal. Although Hal knew that the paper Hightower had published was too dry and academic for a broad audience, he did see a way that the material could be shaped into a book for the general public. He presented his idea to Dr. Hightower, who seemed fully in agreement. He told Hal to write a sample chapter.

Using the professor's paper as a guide, Hal spent the next three weeks writing a rough sample chapter, then presented it to Hightower. Hightower had the chapter for over six weeks, and when he returned it—by mail and with no cover letter—the margins were filled with notes scrawled in red pencil. Many of the notes were in a scolding tone, such as, "Where is your evidence for this?" Or, "This is pure conjecture!" The professor wanted every statement in the chapter substantiated with footnotes. He wanted long quotations inserted, and he wanted Hal to research each idea as he would for a doctoral thesis.

When Hal pointed out to the professor that they were writing a popular book, not an academic thesis, Hightower blew up. He said, "I knew this was going to happen. I simply can't allow you to dilute my research and turn it into one of those awful *National Geographic* specials." When Hal asked Hightower what he meant by this, Hightower cited books such as Carl Sagan's *Cosmos* and Guy Murchie's *The Seven Mysteries of Life*. He complained that such books were "watered down, distorted interpretations of scientific truths," and he would have no part in such an "abomination." Hal argued that such books were not meant to replace scholarly works, but were intended to introduce these subjects to people who might otherwise never know anything about them. Hightower would not hear of this, and he ended the collaboration on the spot, accusing Hal of "attempting to exploit the academic community."

The worst part of this experience for Hal wasn't the personal insult, which he took with a grain of salt, but the fact that Hightower balked at compensating Hal for the three weeks he put into writing the first sample chapter. Eventually Hal did collect from Hightower but only after the matter was referred to an attorney. This hard-earned lesson led to Hal's development of the Stepped Agreement, which helps prevent this kind of misunderstanding from ever reaching the hire-a-lawyer stage.

We don't want to give you the impression that you should sharpen your sword and prepare yourself for the worst, or that you should develop a defensive posture from the beginning. On the contrary, by understanding the kinds of problems that are inherent in collaborative writing, and by knowing what you can do to either avoid or solve those problems before they get out of hand, you can relax and look forward to an exciting and productive association with your collaborator.

PRESERVING THE POWER OF YOUR DREAM

The excitement you experience at the beginning of the project is important. These feelings are not only nice to have but they will be extremely useful as the project moves on. If you take the time to protect the initial positive feelings from the outset, you will be able to go back to them, tap into the excitement you felt, and then use that energy to pull you through the hard times.

Hal recalls the time when he first started writing with a word processor and inadvertently wiped out an entire file containing three days' work. Not having heeded the warnings of the computer experts, he hadn't made a backup file of his work, nor had he printed it up.

There was, of course, nothing to do but rewrite the entire three days' work, reconstructing what he could from memory. Had it not been for the exhilaration he had enjoyed at the beginning of the project, the reconstruction would have been a dull routine. But he was able, time and again, to tap back into his memory of the excitement at the beginning of the project, and his enthusiasm was renewed. Hal felt the rewrite was even better than the original.

Writers—beginners as well as seasoned professionals—sometimes fail to complete projects, not for lack of skill or discipline, but because they fail to pay attention to the "dream," the initial excitement that keeps people motivated. One is here reminded of Thoreau's famous comment on dreams: "If one advances confidently in the direction of his dreams, and endeavors to live the life which he has imagined, he will meet with success unexpected in common hours."

In the initial mental images that are formulated around a project, we often find the "gestalt," that is, a microcosmic vision of the total plan for the completed project. This is not to say that we know, at that point, every detail of the book we are about to write. But we do have the skeleton, the naked armature that can be fleshed out, given muscle and blood, and finally the breath of life, to give a book its special appeal in the marketplace. The birthing process is often a fragile thing that needs sensitive nurturing and care. If there is any single factor that guides this birthing, this fleshing out, this breathing of life into the project, it is the dream.

Do everything possible to keep the dream alive. How do collaborators do that? First, by talking to each other about the dream. Members of athletic teams feel it is their responsibility to keep themselves and their team "psyched up" during a game, talking about how they are going to win right to the end. A similar dynamic is essential for writing teams, fueling their enthusiasm and channeling their work by means of the mutual understanding provided by a Stepped Agreement.

The project and the collaboration are off and running. Your team is ready to make it legal and "go to contract."

ESTABLISHING THE RULES OF THE GAME

The Collaborators' Contract, sometimes called a "Statement of Intent," is a carefully composed document that describes the rights and responsibilities of you and your associate.

In the next few paragraphs, we outline the issues you'll want to consider in this formal contract. (Notice that there is a sample Statement of Intent on pages 99-100, and that not every one of the points described here is necessarily covered in that sample. The reason for this is that each collaboration is unique, and the contract should be tailored to the specific needs of the collaboration. Be flexible, but also take the time to know what the possibilities are—the kinds of issues you can, or should, cover in your contract.)

• The subject of the book, that is, the working title and what the book is about. For example:

> *"We, the undersigned, intend to work together on a book tentatively called* Making Your Fortune In Real Estate, *about buying and selling homes with no money down."*

• A statement about who originated the idea for the book. For example, if you have teamed up with a person who for the past twenty years has been teaching a seminar on the subject, the chances are good that this person will want this stated here:

> *"This book is based on a seminar of the same name, and both parties are in agreement that the teaching seminar is the property of Joe X. Pert, who originated the material."*

If you are working on a novel, this usually won't apply. However, it is conceivable that a person might work out a story line for a novel, and then seek out a writer. In this case, in the working agreement he might want to state who originated the material. If the coauthors have developed a story line together, as a joint effort, that fact can also be stated to avoid conflicts in the future.

• You will want to make a statement about how you will be dividing up the work of writing the book. For example:

> *"Joe X. Pert's main role in producing this book will be to provide research material, written material, and worksheets from his workshop. Ernest Lee Ritten, his coauthor, will do the writing, which he will submit every month for Joe's approval."*

To the above, you might wish to add how you will work together:

> *"We will schedule weekly meetings not to exceed three hours in length, in which we will discuss the progress of the work and share any ideas either of us might have for editorial changes, additions, etc. Prior to the weekly meeting, Ernest Lee Ritten will make certain that Joe X. Pert has received the latest materials and has had time to look them over."*

• Describe any deadlines that apply:

> *"The deadline for the finished manuscript is January 19, 1988."*

• Finally, there should be an agreement of payment—if such payment is to be part of the agreement—and an exact description of the services that will be received for that payment:

> *"Working in the way described above, Ernest Lee Ritten shall receive from Joe X. Pert the total sum of $2,500 for producing a book proposal to include a query letter, a working chapter outline, two sample chapters, and bios on both the expert and the writer."*

Since the Collaborators' Contract is to be a written document, it gives you the ability to go back at any time in the course of your work to refresh your memory (or your partner's) should any disagreement about your rights or responsibilities arise. If you have any doubts about the need for such a written document, consider the fact that people remember details for much less time than the year or more it will take to complete your book. Legal disputes, angry conflicts, or changes in the work agreement that had been mutually agreed upon can be avoided with a written document.

A word of caution: If you get involved with a collaborator who is not clear about the book he or she wishes to write, you may put in many hours helping that person to brainstorm and clarify the purpose of the book.

On two projects with which he has been involved, Hal established a consulting arrangement with an expert coauthor because that person was not yet clear about what he wanted to say. In one case, Hal put in over 200 consulting hours, over a two year period, before his coauthor was able to make a definitive statement about the book he wished to write. It would have been prohibitive for Hal to put in so many hours on the defining stage except that the expert knew the value of this consulting service and was willing to pay for it.

SAMPLE STATEMENT OF INTENT:
ONE FORM OF A COLLABORATORS' CONTRACT

The following is a letter that defines one working relationship and the division of earnings for a book whose core idea grew out of a management training program developed by one of the coauthors. Written in the form of a letter, it is just one way to write a Collaborators' Contract.

(Date)
(From)
(To)

Dear Thomas:

The following is a description of the working relationship
we discussed for writing *The Book*. Look it over and make
any changes or corrections you feel are necessary. If no
changes are necessary, just sign it and send me back my
copy.

1. We understand that I will need a total of $15,000 to
write the book.

2. We will each receive 50 percent of the advance. For
purposes of calculating my time, I will keep a time sheet of
hours, charged at the rate of $30 per hour.

3. We will take out a joint copyright on the book; your
name will be given top billing on the book cover; my name
will be in smaller type, appearing with the conjunction
"with."

4. I understand that the program upon which the book is
based is your sole property.

5. The working relationship we will follow will be as
described here: I will do all of the finished writing, working
from materials you have already provided, and which you
will provide as we go along. We will schedule four-hour
meetings every two weeks, during which I will ask you
questions and/or we will discuss the book. I will send you
each chapter as it is completed, for you to read and return
with corrections. Rewrites will be handled in the same way.

6. Should there be difficulties between us which affect the
production of the book, and which we cannot solve on our
own, we will share in the cost of hiring a facilitator we both
agree on to help us resolve our conflicts.

7. Should one or both of us wish to dissolve this working agreement:

(a) There will be a settlement of any outstanding costs, such as paying back publisher's advances.
(b) The writer (name) shall keep any money received for services rendered.
(c) A dissolution notice will not be considered binding until we both agree to the terms of the dissolution.

Let me know how all this sounds to you. I'm looking forward to getting started on the project.

Yours truly,
(Signature of writer)
(Signature of collaborator)

WHO'S ON FIRST?

Remember the classic Abbot and Costello routine with the comedians struggling to communicate the names of the players on a baseball team? Sometimes, collaborations can sound like that, with coauthors struggling to decide who is supposed to be doing what.

What are the choices in deciding who is boss—or if there is a boss? What if you discover that your collaborator/expert views writers as little more than glorified secretaries who "take dictation and polish up a few phrases?" Or what about collaborators who want you to take all the risks, while they sit back and wait for you and the publisher to make them rich and famous? You may think this sounds like a gross exaggeration, but unfortunately we are describing people we have had to deal with. People who don't write often have wild expectations about what it takes to produce a book, and the better prepared you are to set limits that you know will work for you, and the more ready you are to reject what won't work for you, the better off you're going to be.

Take the case of a busy physician who once contacted Hal to write a book for him. After an initial meeting in the physician's home, Hal spent two hours putting together a tentative book proposal based on one of the doctor's ideas. Hal mailed these off and a week later received a call from the doctor's secretary to set up a date for a second meeting. On the day of that meeting, Hal started off by discussing his fees for consulting time and writing. When the doctor heard that Hal wanted money for his work, rather than waiting for the book itself to start earning, he dug in his heels and stopped the project.

"I figure it this way," the doctor said. "I am contributing my medical credentials to the project. My time is worth over $150 per hour. Since you charge so much less for your time, you should be paying me to help you write the book!"

The doctor wanted his name featured on the cover; he wanted his ideas followed to the letter; and he felt that he was due 90 percent of the earnings. What he failed to see is that writers, too, are professionals, whose educations span a lifetime. They have families to raise, rent to pay, and the need for vacations.

Creative people tend to undervalue their services. This may be because, for many of them, the creative process itself is reward enough. We simply can't imagine getting paid for doing something we enjoy so much. Unfortunately, there are those who are more than willing to exploit that self-effacing quality of the writer, and writers who allow themselves to be used this way really do a great disservice to the profession.

When pricing your services, remind yourself and your collaborator that you are a professional. To become a writer takes as many years of hard work as it takes to become a lawyer or doctor or business person. "Everyone writes," Somerset Maugham once said. "But only a rare few ever become writers."

Put a price on your time. Depending on your experience and publishing record, that might be anything from $10 an hour to $120 an hour.

When you're putting together a working agreement with a coauthor, also keep in mind that you'll be working with other people: agents, editors, and publishers. The more people involved, the more room there is for error which, if you're not careful, can end up costing you money.

A publisher once asked Hal if he would be interested in working with a well-known lecturer who was under contract with him. Hal was offered 50 percent of the royalties, with a 50 percent advance against royalties. The publisher told Hal he would receive a $15,000 advance. Hal met with his coauthor, liked him, and the two men agreed to work together. Contracts were signed and a young editor was assigned to the project.

The publisher told Hal that he would sit down with his editor and tell her exactly what he expected from the book. This was unusual. Publishers do not ordinarily direct the writing to this extent. But these were special circumstances. The publisher had given the lecturer a contract without first seeing a proposal. A year later, with no book or proposal in sight, the publisher put on the pressure only to discover that the lecturer didn't have the time to write the book. Hal was learning the real truth only in bits and pieces, and only after he had signed the contract to write the book.

On the first meeting with the editor, Hal was handed a stack of books, including the work of Napolean Hill, Og Mandino, and others from the success book genre. The editor erroneously told Hal that this was the kind of book the publisher wanted. On the basis of that advice, Hal spent the following month developing a book outline and sample chapter. He submitted this work and a week later received an insulting letter from the publisher, saying that Hal apparently didn't understand the assignment and that he was scheduling a hard work session between his editor and Hal to straighten things out.

Bewildered by the publisher's response, Hal tried to reach him by phone but was told only that he would get all the information he needed after meeting with the editor. At the editorial meeting, Hal was once again reminded of the success books he'd been given on the previous meeting. He was told that he should follow them as models for the book he was writing. Later, sitting down with the notes from that meeting, Hal put in another week's work rewriting the sample chapter, attempting to refine the style presented in the books the editor had given him. When this work was submitted once again, another nasty note came back from the publisher, this time threatening to take Hal off the job.

Hal called the publisher, and this time insisted on talking to him rather than to the editor. When Hal described the editorial meetings, and told how the editor had presented him with the success books, insisting that the book be written in that style, the publisher flew into a rage. "That is not what I want at all," he said. As it turned out, he wanted the language to be inspirational, as in many of the better success books, but he wanted the meat of the book to be presented through facts and anecdotes.

This time around, Hal produced a working outline and sample chapter that satisfied the publisher. And although apologies were made for the misunderstanding, it still cost Hal more than six weeks of his time, for which he was not immediately compensated. Eventually, justice was served, however; Hal earned several thousand dollars in royalties past the original advance, and the editor who had caused the confusion was fired.

Do whatever you can to avoid problems like these. But no one is infallible. There is as much room for error in publishing as in any business. Editors change in the middle of books, and the new editors may bring an entirely new perspective to a project. Contracts are contracts in publishing, and the main responsibility of the writer is to produce an *acceptable* book. "Acceptable" is one of those words that leaves a lot of room for interpretation. It means a manuscript that the publisher likes and can sell. If he doesn't get that, the writer may end up spending weeks or even months rewriting the manuscript.

Expect that rewrites will be necessary. Make certain that your coauthor understands this and is willing to share the burden of rewrites with you, be it in sitting down and sharing the work equally with you or by compensating you financially.

It is nearly impossible to write a Collaborators' Contract that covers all possibilities. For that reason, there is no substitute for trust and good faith between you and your collaborator. One thing that can help establish this good faith is for both of you to understand the risks as well as the rewards of writing. To do this, we recommend that after your initial contact, you lend this book to your collaborator.

Agents you work with should also have a complete picture of how to put collaborations together—and keep them together! At the very least, discuss what you have learned here with your agent. You might even take the book along to your meetings, flagging the pages that cover material you think is relevant, and using the book as a reference to make certain you can work together effectively.

Find out if there are important disparities between your way of thinking and that of your prospective writing partner or agent. Small disparities may be easily negotiated at this point. If you are realistic in your expectations, but can't get what you want, now is the time to look for a fresh start with a collaborator, or agent, or both, whose views are more to your liking.

EQUAL PARTNERS,
LIMITED PARTNERS,
OR GHOST FOR HIRE?

There are three basic categories of working relationships—equal partners, limited partners, and ghost for hire—to consider:

Equal Partners: (Not to be confused with "partnership," which is a legal term with other meanings.) This is the situation when you and your writing partner agree to work as full partners—sharing equally in everything. This means that you both agree to contribute equally to the writing of the book, and that you will share equally in all income derived from it. You share the risks and the financial rewards equally.

Limited Partners: This is when you and your collaborator have different rights and responsibilities. Such partnerships can become extremely complicated. For example, for several years, Peter Harrington taught a real estate seminar on buying and selling residential properties. He had worked out a system for doing this and had developed a program for a teaching system.

Few people would dispute that the program he had developed was his rightful property. Yet he became involved with a writer who, after getting a hundred pages into the book, informed Peter that he expected to receive 50 percent of any income earned by the book. Peter was outraged and wisely pulled out of the project, forfeiting more than $2,000 he had advanced his writer.

Peter was a sharp businessman, yet he had allowed himself to get a hundred pages into the book before defining the relationship with his writer. But book collaborations are a world unto themselves, one that few people outside the business understand.

Eventually Peter found a literary agent who put him together with a collaborator and helped him obtain an equitable deal. The writer, a professional who knew his business as well as he knew his craft, saw that Peter had developed a complete program that required little more than writing skill to turn into a book. He asked for and got a generous flat fee for his own contribution to the book, with a 10 percent share of the royalties after the first 30,000 books sold.

In his years as a book collaborator and author, Hal has worked with a variety of collaborators. The agreements he has made run the gamut from verbal agreements over supper with his friend Mike Samuels—with whom he has coauthored four successful books—to his agent-negotiated contract with a world-renowned athlete whose contact with him consisted of one three-hour meeting at a hotel. Hal's experience proves that every collaboration needs to be approached in a different way.

Limited partnerships are applicable in those situations where you are working with a person who already has an idea, a program, or perhaps—as in the case of an autobiography—a life story to tell. As the writer, you can hardly make equal claim to those things, but as a writer, you do have a right to claim "ownership" of the experience, skills, and work that you will invest in shaping the material into a book.

As a writer, is your rightful portion of the book's proceeds 10 percent? 25 percent? 50 percent? Or should you get a flat fee for your contribution?

Part of the riddle about figuring your portion of the proceeds may be found in considering who is taking the financial risks. If, for example, your coauthor puts up money for you to write the book, or gives you a larger portion of the publisher's advance so that you can devote your full time to the writing, you should expect to forfeit some or all of the royalties.

The trade-off between immediate payment and royalties isn't necessarily a bad one, but be careful not to give too much away in your haste to get down to work. Weigh your options before you sign anything. Here are a few of the possibilities:

• Hal once had a client who hired him to take her doctoral thesis and rewrite it in a popular style. She planned to self-publish this book and sell it at seminars, which she taught throughout the world. Hal charged a flat fee for his services, with no royalty clause.

• Dennis Parker, a professional writer who specializes in helping people develop workshops for the business community, charges his clients a flat fee of $7,500 for writing a workbook and training materials. His contract gives him 3 percent of all income from each workshop. At $290 per person for a two-day workshop, this small royalty provides decent profits for this writer.

• When Michael Larsen and his partner Elizabeth Pomada wrote *Daughters Of Painted Ladies,* they agreed to share their earnings equally, after their agents had deducted their commissions. They paid their photographer a flat fee.

Ghost for Hire: In some ways the simplest working agreement you can make is that of the "hired gun," or "ghost for hire." In this situation, the writer works for an hourly rate or a flat fee. The writer may keep a time sheet and periodically submit a statement of hours for payment.

But don't forget that even a ghost-for-hire can request "perks," payment beyond the hourly rate should the book do well in the marketplace. For example, you might write into your collaboration agreement a clause that says you will receive a "bonus" of a certain amount of money should the book sell over a certain number of copies.

In some cases, there may be a possibility of earning income from subsidiary rights: reprints in magazines of portions of your book, film rights, rights for videocassettes or "other electronic media" (forms of recording or reproduction yet to be invented). Although film rights are generally associated with novels, don't forget that subjects such as history, anthropology, biography, and nature lend themselves to production for documentaries, television mini-series, and educational films and television. Shares in all these should be considered in the negotiation of any writing contract. In some cases, income from these categories can exceed the income from the book, as Michael once learned in selling film rights to a manuscript for a novel that, as it turned out, was never published as a book.

The details for working out publishing contracts are beyond the scope of this book. For more information on this subject, we recommend Richard Balkin's book *How to Understand and Negotiate a Book Contract or Magazine Agreement.*

SUMMARY—THE THREE R'S

Though working out the details of your collaboration may sound complicated, the only question you really need ask is: "How are the Risks, Rights, and Responsibilities going to be divided?"

- Is this truly an *equal* partnership, or is one or the other partner making a larger contribution?

- How are ideas for the book going to be generated? From whom do the ideas come, and who will *own* those ideas? Will one of the partners be earning income from lecturing on the content of the book?

- If there is a teaching program involved in the book project, to whom does that program belong?

- What percentage of the writing will each of you do? Will you be doing 50 percent? 75 percent? 100 percent?

- If there is going to be research involving libraries, telephone calls, interviews, or travel, who will be responsible for doing that research, and who will pay for it?

- If photography or artwork is involved, who will pay for it?

- Who will pay for typing, postage, photocopying, etc?

- How will royalties and other income from the book be divided?

- If the responsibilities change as you go along—for example, if your collaborator, who is also a lecturer, has increased commitments on the lecture circuit, leaving you alone to write the book—how will the two of you handle that?

You need not answer every one of these questions, but discuss these issues with your collaborator. Make it clear that you know how to put together a working agreement, and that you have knowledge in defining working relationships. If nothing else, this will establish you as a professional in your collaborator's mind, which helps both of you get started on a solid footing.

WHERE'S THE BOOK?

So far, we've focused on the business end of the collaboration, how the two of you will work together. Now let's turn to the contents of the book itself, and focus on producing a rough outline. This rough outline (step three in the Stepped Agreement) will be the basis for the material you'll include in the book proposal. It will consist of the following:

1. A single paragraph describing what the book is about. For example:

    Making Your Fortune in Real Estate *is written for every person who thinks it is too late to make big money in the real estate market. It shows how, with little or no money down, you can turn a big profit by buying and selling residential properties.*

2. A chapter outline, consisting of chapter titles and one or two-line descriptions of each. For example:

    CHAPTER OUTLINE
    Chapter 1: Creating Your Estate with $500 Down—This is a motivational chapter, consisting of anecdotes that illustrate how there is money to be made in real estate—regardless of how much capital you have.
    Chapter 2: Taking Inventory of Your Assets—This chapter begins with a challenge to the reader, with a checklist of the qualities and financial resources you need to succeed in real estate.

3. A brief market analysis, consisting of a description of the reader to whom the book is aimed, a short list of books presently available to indicate that there is an established market for your book, and a statement telling how your book offers something new for this market. For example:

    Books such as Joe Smith's Making Millions In Real Estate, *and John Jones'* There's A Fortune In Buying And Selling

Foreclosure Properties, *have each sold over two million copies in the four years since their publication. My book,* Making Your Fortune In Real Estate, *addresses the same readership—the person with little or no startup capital and limited experience in the real estate market. What makes my book unique is that it introduces three new models for developing financial assets that will qualify the reader to bid on houses up for FHA and other foreclosure auctions.*

How you do the above will depend, in part, on the working relationship you've defined. For example, if you have decided upon an equal partnership, you and your partner will be working together, or at least spending the same amount of time, producing the outline. If, on the other hand, you are ghosting the book, you may be alone in producing the outline. In the first example, no money changes hands because both authors are contributing equal time and effort. In the second situation, the writer is doing the work alone, and should be paid by the "author."

If you have discussed the book, or have had an opportunity to look over articles or research materials the other person has collected, or even a rough manuscript or a workbook, you should be able to write a rough outline of the kind described above in four to six hours. If you are doing the writing without the help of the other person, and if the agreement you have is that you will be working on an hourly basis, keep track of your time and charge accordingly. In any case, the time for this work should be charged according to the formula you have worked out in the Stepped Agreement.

The outline you produce has two purposes: First, it will function as a focal point, allowing you and your collaborator to discuss your ideas on the book and to make certain that you are seeing eye to eye. A written document leaves little room for misunderstanding. Second, it allows you to get to know your collaborator a little better, and to bow out if you run into a major snag.

As you work with your collaborator, you may have to make revisions of your original outline. Keep a record of your time, make revisions you can both agree upon, and prepare a fresh outline. Send this outline to your collaborator, along with a letter describing how you will proceed. Include the following:

• A paragraph telling the collaborator that you have enclosed a copy of the revisions you made together on the outline, and that you would like him or her to read over these revisions, make any further revisions, and mail them back to you.

• A paragraph saying that if your collaborator agrees, you will now write a proposal to submit to the publisher.

• A statement at the bottom of the page, with a blank space for a date and your collaborator's signature, with a request that he or she sign the enclosed letter and send it back to you as a way to acknowledge the agreement with you on the outline. This signature is also an agreement to proceed with the project as you have described.

SUMMARY AND MOVING AHEAD

By now, you have accomplished the following:

• You have blocked out the getting-acquainted process with a Stepped Agreement.

• As part of the Stepped Agreement, you have written a rough book outline, giving you a clear picture of the book and further testing your working relationship with your collaborator.

• You have a statement from your collaborator, approving your rough outline, giving you the go-ahead to write the proposal, and approving your terms for that work.

• You have formulated a collaboration contract that defines who is working for or with whom—stating the risks and responsibilities of both you and your collaborator.

You are now ready to write the proposal.

WRITING THE BOOK PROPOSAL

The time you will need to write a proposal will vary, depending on your experience, your familiarity with the material, the nature of the book, and your own writing habits. Hal, who has written more than thirty book proposals, estimates between 100 and 150 hours to write a thirty to seventy page proposal that includes up to two sample chapters. If the book is on a subject that is new to you, the person with whom you are working should either submit material to you in a form that you and the publisher can understand, or be willing to pay you to become familiar with the subject through your own study.

THE PARTS OF A NONFICTION BOOK PROPOSAL

One of the tasks of a nonfiction writing team will be to write a selling proposal for the book. This will consist of the following elements. Arm your proposal with as much ammunition as you can that will help catch the editor's attention and sell the book. For more ammunition than we can include in this short outline, see Michael Larsen's book, *How To Write a Book Proposal*, from which this was adapted. Among the things to be covered in the proposal are:

I. INTRODUCTION
Include a short description of what the book is about; segments of the public which you feel will be interested in buying your book (grade school teachers, general readers, people between the ages of 26 and 40 who want to improve their marriage, etc.); other books on the subject, and how yours is different and better; the length of the book in manuscript pages; what the authors will do to help promote the book; and short third person bios of the authors, including only what will impress the editor (relevant credentials, previous publishing histories, if any, and what qualifies the authors to write this book).

II. THE CHAPTER-BY-CHAPTER OUTLINE
Your outline should include from a paragraph to a page of information for every chapter, telling enough to excite an editor and provide a clear picture about each chapter's contents.

III. SAMPLE CHAPTERS
Editors like to see at least one, and preferably two sample chapters; one if the chapters will cover different material in the same way

(for example, a guidebook of ten cities); and at least 10 percent of the manuscript if, like an encyclopedia, the book won't be structured in chapters.

AGENT OR NO AGENT?
TWO ALTERNATIVES FOR SELLING
A PROPOSAL

Without an Agent

If, for one reason or another, you aren't working with an agent, you may wish to send your proposal directly to the publisher. In that case, there are five steps for acting as your own agent.

1. Research which publishing houses are publishing books on topics similar to yours. For example, let's say that you are writing a book on automobile repair. Look for publishers who already have a list of similar books. It indicates not only that they might be looking for more books in that general area, but that their marketing department would be aware of how to reach the readers for whom your book is intended.

If your book is nonfiction, begin this research by browsing through the bookstores, looking for books in the same subject area as yours, and then noting the names of publishers who you feel match up with your needs. If your book is a work of fiction, look for publishers who are prominently publishing the type of fiction you're writing. For example, not all publishers publish *literary* works of fiction; some publish only *genre* fiction, such as romances, thrillers, or science fiction.

Consult a copy of *Writer's Market* or *Literary Market Place*. These books give you brief descriptions of each publisher, telling what they publish, names, addresses, phone numbers, and the names of editors. Both are available at public libraries.

2. Call one or more publishing houses and ask for the Editor-in-Chief. You will get his or her assistant. Ask for the names of editors who do the kind of book you're proposing. If more than one does, ask who will be the best for your book.

3. Send a one-page query letter describing what your book is about and why you think it is different and better than anything else on the market. Close the letter by asking the editor if he or she would like to see a complete proposal. Enclose a self-addressed stamped postcard, with boxes on the back the editors can check to tell you whether or not to submit the proposal.

4. Some publishers won't accept simultaneous submissions, that is, submissions of your query letter or proposal sent to several publishers at the same time. However, it is not unusual for a publisher to take several weeks to respond to a query letter, and several months to make a decision on a proposal. Considering that many proposals see the desks of twenty or more publishers before they're published, one can see that a writer could spend many months, or even years, getting a book published if the single-submission etiquette was followed.

Before making simultaneous submissions, do a little research. *Writer's Market* publishes information about which publishers accept simultaneous submissions. First submit to those who do accept them. Then, if there are publishers who don't accept such submissions, but to whom you would like to submit, write to them, tell them what you're doing, and ask if they would like to see what you have to offer. Give them the option of looking at your work now or after the other publishers have replied.

When making simultaneous submissions, never send photocopies of queries or cover letters. Send each editor an original typed or computer-printed copy.

5. When responses to your queries arrive, you're in business. You can send good quality photocopies of the proposal (for non-fiction and genre fiction) or the complete manuscript (for fiction). Send each one with an individually typed letter, referring to their last letter to you requesting to see the proposal. In addition to your SASE, enclose a self-addressed stamped postcard, with boxes the editors can check to indicate the date they received the manuscript and the date you can expect a response. (Keep returned cards on file. If you haven't heard from the editor by the time indicated, give him or her a phone call.)

Be sure to keep careful records of where you've sent query letters and proposals.

With an Agent

Having completed the proposal or the complete novel, send a high-quality photocopy of it to your agent. (If you're wondering how to get an agent, see *Literary Agents: How to Get and Work with the Right One for You*, by Michael Larsen.)

If visual materials such as photos or artwork are part of the project, include samples. One approach for showing how you will integrate the text and illustrations is to include the illustrations for the sample chapters. The more important the artwork is to your book, the more important it is to include samples. Never send original artwork. Use photocopies, duplicate slides, or color prints.

If you have not yet established a working relationship with the agent, send the same one-page query letter and postcard you would send to an editor.

If you have already established an ongoing working relationship with an agent, he or she will usually make comments on the proposal, returning it to you with suggestions for changes.

If you have not established a working relationship with the agent, one of two things can happen: The proposal may be rejected and returned to you with little or no comment, or the agent will contact you and make an appointment to discuss how you might work together.

AGENTS' CONTRACTS

On the subject of agents for collaborative writing, one of the first questions people ask is this: "Is it necessary for the collaborators to have the same agent?" The answer is no, but the fewer people involved in negotiating a contract, the easier it's going to be. Several times over the years, Hal has written books with collaborators who lived in different towns, and who had different agents. Moreover, one agent lived in New York while the other did business from San Francisco. There were no major problems with this, other than the fact that all communications had to be sent to four different people at four different locations.

If your agents are pros, they are accustomed to working with people all over the country. Each day their time is spent

talking on the phone, having meetings, and looking over correspondence with writers, publishers, editors, and other agents.
Beyond this, the following are the four most common questions
people ask about their associations with literary agents:

Q #1. What is an agent's customary fee in a collaboration?
A. The same as it is for the agent of any writer—10 or 15 percent of any money the book earns for the author(s).

Q #2. Do both collaborators have to pay the 15 percent fee?
A. The agent receives 15 percent of the authors' total earnings on a book, regardless of how you and your coauthor divide
your own earnings. If you and your collaborator have different
agents, the total commissions paid to agents is still only 15 percent of the total earnings of the book.

There are exceptions to the above rule. For example, if you
are ghosting the book for a flat fee, have *not* gotten the job
through an agent, and your collaborator is paying you directly,
you would not have a contract with a literary agent and would
therefore not pay any agent's commissions.

Q #3. Is it customary for agents to ask for a contract between
themselves and the writers they represent?
A. Yes. The reasons for this are numerous: First, the agents
invest time, money in postage and telephone calls, and their own
reputations to sell your proposal. The contract makes it clear to
you both that you will not have a second agent representing the
same book—leading to embarrassment for all concerned should
two copies of the same proposal end up on the same publisher's
desk, represented by two different agents who do not know
about each other! When collaborators have different agents,
those agents work together, coordinating their work so that
there will be no duplication. Both authors should know what the
agreement between the agents is, so that they can follow up if
any problems arise.

Q #4. Should I expect my agent to help me work out a contract with my collaborator?
A. Not necessarily. Your agent may have a contract that you
can use. If not, ask the agent to review the contract you and your
collaborator work out, to make certain it is fair to you. The agent

may help you negotiate a 50-50 contract, if you are working as an equal partner with your collaborator. He may also help you negotiate a ghosting contract. If the agreement is long or complicated, the agent may refer you to a literary attorney. As a professional collaborator, you will take the lead in setting up working agreements with coauthors.

CONTRACT CONSIDERATIONS

The contract you sign with a publisher should reflect the agreement you made with your collaborator. If you have an equal partnership with your collaborator, sharing responsibilities and income from the project equally, your publishing contract should contain your name as well as the name of your collaborator. Usually this means that both coauthors' names will appear in the spaces naming the author(s). On the other end of the spectrum, if you are ghosting a book, your name may or may not appear in the publisher's contract. Here are some of the ways ghosting contracts are written:

• You have a contract directly with your coauthor, and that person agrees to pay a flat fee directly to you. It is customary to agree to a flat fee for the job, which should be specified in a contract (See Appendix E), but the total sum is paid in increments. For example, you may be paid half on signing and half when the manuscript is accepted by an editor. Or you may be paid on a monthly basis. Personal preference applies here. Collaborators may decide to keep an accounting of hours spent writing, with payment based on a weekly or monthly timesheet. Or the same accounting and payment might be based on a per-page rate.

• Your literary agent sets up the contract between you and your collaborator.

• Perks and bonuses—earnings over and above a flat fee earned by a writer—may be described in a separate written agreement with your coauthor or in an amendment to the contract your coauthor holds with the publishers. These may be spelled out on a separate page attached to the publisher's contract.

When there is an agent involved, payments from publisher to writer are made through the agent. In other words, contracts involving an agent will stipulate that the publisher pays the agent. The agent is responsible for making sure that the income received is correct and for dispersing the funds to the author or authors, after deducting agency commissions. At tax time, your agent will send you withholding statements. The advantages are that the agent is relatively objective and can help settle conflicts. In addition, the bookkeeping records can become fairly complex, and letting the agent do it means there's one less thing you have to deal with.

Limited working relationships, such as ghostwriting arrangements, may or may not involve the publishing contract. For example, assume that you and your coauthor have agreed that you will receive 75 percent of the author's advance so that you can devote your full time to writing the book. You further agree that you will receive 25 percent of any royalties paid the author after the sale of 100,000 copies of the book. If this money is to be paid out of funds received from the publisher, your agreement should be stated in the publisher's contract so that an agent, or the publisher if you are not working with an agent, can keep a clear accounting of the disbursement of any payments. If you have an agreement to receive bonuses, there should also be a stipulation that you will receive a copy of the semi-annual royalty statements so you can keep track of the book's income. In some cases, of course, limited working relationships are spelled out in contracts between coauthors, and the publisher may never even be aware that there is a second writer involved. In such cases, your name will not even appear in the publisher's contract, but you will have a contract with your coauthor.

AND, WITH, OR AS TOLD TO

There are many ways to indicate your author's credit or by-line on the cover of a book. The most frequently used conjunctions are *and,* *with,* and *as told to.* When authors are to be considered as equals, it is customary to use "and" or no conjunction at all.

Usually the first name on the cover is considered to be the more important. If, for example, the book is on a medical subject, written by an M.D. with a person who has no medical credentials, the name of the person with the credentials would usually come first, since the book buyer would be looking for them. The same is true where a noted authority or famous person is a coauthor with a person who is not well-known. When authorship is equal, the names may be listed alphabetically, the authors may flip a coin to decide whose name will appear first, see which order sounds best, or decide through some other method of their own devising. The following will help you decide how your names should appear:

Use the Conjunction:	To Indicate That:
And or no conjunction	The collaboration is a true coauthorship, with both people contributing equally. Most frequently used for fiction or nonfiction works where the collaborators feel they are both *authors.*
With	The person whose name follows was the writer, while the name appearing first is the subject of, or expert for the book. Most frequently used when one person plays a lesser role, functioning only as writer or research assistant.
As Told To	The person whose name follows acted as a "scribe," taking down the story of the person whose name comes first. Most frequently used in biographies and eyewitness accounts.

UNLIMITED POSSIBILITIES

It is impossible in a book addressed to the broad scope of collaborative writing to cover all the possible contract situations you might encounter.

In the model we provide in the Appendix, royalties are paid to the author on a royalty basis: for example, the contract might state that the author receives 10 percent of the retail cover price of $17.95, or $1.795.

Coauthors, of course, share in the amounts they receive from advances, royalties, and subsidiary rights. Usually the rights of coauthors are spelled out in "riders," or typewritten amendments added to the contract. Riders may include: how the coauthor's name will appear on the book; in whose name the copyright will be registered; copyrights for artwork or photography that are held by one of the coauthors and registered as separate properties; who will be responsible for paying the coauthor (publisher, author, or agent); and perhaps whether the coauthor will be expected to participate (or specifically not participate) in the promotion of the book.

If you don't have an agent, know enough about contracts to make certain you get what you should be getting. But to make certain that you know what you are getting, get the help of a literary agent or an attorney who is well versed in publishing contracts. Not all attorneys are, so make certain you know whom you're dealing with.

Literary attorneys are in short supply outside New York, and though it is always better to work with someone you can meet with, experience is preferable to proximity. You can obtain the name of an attorney from national writers' and agents' organizations or through the following referral services:

Volunteer Lawyers for the Arts
36 W. 44th St.
New York, NY 10036
(212) 575-1150

Bay Area Lawyers for the Arts
Room 255, Building C
Fort Mason, San Francisco, CA 94123
(415) 775-7200

Lawyers for the Creative Arts
111 N. Wabash Ave.
Chicago, IL 60602
(312) 263-6989

You may also wish to check *The Legal Directory* in your local library for lists of lawyers in your area who specialize in literary laws.

8

A WRITER'S WORK IS NEVER DONE

Stories of legendary editors like Max Perkins, who discovered and encouraged some of America's greatest literary heroes—Thomas Wolfe, F. Scott Fitzgerald, Ernest Hemingway, Ring Lardner, and James Jones—are rare. Perkins was an extraordinary editor who worked closely with his authors, and was able to see the genius of writers whose work might have been overlooked by other editors.

In A. Scott Berg's biography, *Max Perkins: Editor of Genius*, there is a photo of Thomas Wolfe standing over a wooden box containing the more than 3,000 pages of manuscript he brought to Perkins to publish. The picture recalls the stories that made Perkins a legend in publishing, reminding us that it was this editor who invested hundreds of hours of his own time shaping this writer's work into publishable novels. Without Perkins' effort, the chances are good that the world would never have enjoyed the talents of this great American novelist.

It was also Perkins who encouraged F. Scott Fitzgerald's literary career, and it was Perkins' loyalty and deep friendship that supported Fitzgerald, both financially and emotionally, through the last years of the novelist's life. One wonders if Fitzgerald, whose life was marked by a difficult and tragic marriage, bouts with alcoholism, and self-doubts about his talent, would have been as productive as he was without Perkins' friendship and support.

No other editor has done as much for American literature.

121

Perkins' colorful career is etched with stories that show how deeply he became involved in the lives of the writers he worked with. One sees him striding through the streets of Greenwich Village beside Thomas Wolfe, who boisterously recites long passages from his books, his voice echoing through the empty city streets at 2 A.M. Or one sees him lounging on a white beach at Ernest Hemingway's home in Cuba, poring over that writer's latest manuscript. Or one sees him on the phone in his own office in Manhattan, talking Fitzgerald, who is in Europe, through a creative dry spell, with Fitzgerald convinced that his talent has abandoned him forever.

Stories like these establish a romantic ideal in our minds that perhaps will never be erased. How easy writing would be with a Max Perkins in one's life! The trouble is that while we hold such ideals in our minds, dreaming that our own Max Perkins will discover our hidden talent and nurse it out into the open, into books, the years slip by and our ideas never get beyond ideas.

As romantic and wonderful as Max Perkins' legend may be, we do ourselves a disservice by clinging to the ideals he represents instead of looking at the hard realities of today's publishing world and then getting down to business. Once you recognize those hard realities, you may find them quite manageable after all.

For unpublished writers, and sometimes for published ones, agents and editors may seem remote and elusive, difficult if not impossible to reach. For the most part this, too, is part of the myth that works against everyone—writer, agent, editor, and publisher. One should never forget that editors and agents make their livelihoods finding books to publish. They need you more than you need them. Without writers, agents have no manuscripts to take to publishers, publishers have no books to publish, and booksellers nothing to sell. If you have a publishable proposal or manuscript, you have the ticket you need to get an agent or editor.

Keep in mind that each year the publishing world puts out between 35,000 and 50,000 new titles. This means that every year there are that many opportunities for your book to be published.

For every 35,000 books published, ten times that many

manuscripts or proposals are making the rounds of editors and agents. How can you possibly compete with such numbers? The answer might surprise you. You compete by being professional in everything you do to get your idea across. Your professionalism will get you noticed, will make your efforts highly visible in the mountain of unpublishable manuscripts that come to editors in the mail.

Above all, approach your writing as a business. You and your collaborator may have the ideas and be doing the writing, but when you submit a manuscript to major publishers, don't forget that you are asking them to invest more than $50,000 in overhead, editorial time, author's advance, and first printing.

Every day editors and agents receive manuscripts and proposals that are poorly typed (even handwritten!), that have misspellings and marginal notes too confusing to decipher, and that are so badly put together that they communicate nothing more than naivete at best, and complete disregard for the reader at worst. If there is a book idea in them, it is too densely camouflaged to be found.

Agents' and editors' mailbags disgorge book proposals that show little or no knowledge of the book business and the art of proposal writing. Agents and editors pass over hundreds of good book ideas submitted to them each year because they don't have the time or the stomach for struggling through unprofessional presentations. But the really sad part is that the information for making professional presentations is readily available to writers, through articles in magazines such as *Writers Digest,* and through books on manuscript preparation, proposal writing, working with an agent, and editing. These are skills that you can learn. The keys to a successful writing career are within easy reach. The style of your writing and your professionalism in presenting your work are essential criteria for busy editors and agents, and it will often be for want of this professionalism that perfectly salable projects are rejected.

Regard your agent and publisher as business partners and associates. Accord them the attention to detail and respect for their time that you would extend to any person or institution you wanted to gamble more than $50,000 on a business proposition. This perspective will serve you well; it's the reality you face.

SPECIAL CONSIDERATIONS FOR COLLABORATORS

Most of the things that apply to people writing alone also apply to collaborative writers. You must produce a professional proposal or manuscript. Follow guidelines in books such as *The Elements of Style, The Chicago Manual Of Style,* and Michael's *How To Write A Book Proposal.*

You should know, however, that many publishers don't read manuscripts or book proposals that come in "over the transom," that is, unsolicited. Because of their busy schedules, editors at major houses depend on agents to separate the wheat from the chaff, winnowing out manuscripts that show no promise, and delivering only those projects that are in a professional form, and that contain ideas worth the time and effort required to present them to an editorial board. In this respect, although they are paid by authors, agents have come to function as front-line editors for publishing houses.

WHO DOES WHAT: RESPONSIBILITIES AND ETIQUETTE

How much help can you expect from an agent in "packaging" your book idea? If you get an agent's attention through a phone call or query letter, and then follow up with a manuscript or proposal, you can expect a careful reading of your work. If your work needs to be put into a more salable form, an agent will make suggestions on how to do it. Most agents do not do editorial work, or if they do, you should expect to pay for their efforts. If your agent doesn't do this kind of work, he or she may be able to tell you where to get the editorial help you need to develop your proposal or manuscript. But you are responsible for getting your work into salable form.

In the process of selling a manuscript, agents negotiate contracts for the authors they represent. They may give some free general counsel and advice along the way. However, many agents will want you to work out collaborative agreements—contracts between you and your writing partner—on your own. Such an agreement, frequently drawn up by a literary attorney, is suggested or even required by publishers. This protects them from getting into the middle of a dispute between you and your coauthor.

It is best if both writers sit in on all meetings with agents or editors. However, it may not always be possible to get everyone together for every meeting. If you don't work together in this way, there's room for error and conflict between writers, editors, and the four or five people who get involved in the production of your book. Avoid miscommunication at all costs. Imagine what can happen if one collaborator simply misinterprets details of a meeting he has had with an agent or editor.

Hal once worked with a collaborator who was on the national lecture circuit. The lecturer, whom we shall call Dr. Gnu Etal, had a contract with a publisher for a book based on a motivational lecture for which he was famous. Hal had been hired by the publisher and it was his responsibility to produce a working outline and then write the book. Hal and Dr. Gnu Etal produced a working chapter outline and submitted it to the publisher in New York. The publisher gave his okay and, while Dr. Gnu Etal was on the road, Hal proceeded to start work on chapter three, since the research was not yet complete on the first two chapters.

While in New York, Dr. Gnu Etal had lunch with the editor and the two men made what they believed to be minor changes in the chapter outline. They decided to cut chapter three and incorporate it into two other chapters. When Dr. Gnu Etal returned to his hotel room that night, he received a phone call from his secretary informing him of an error in his schedule, necessitating that he get on a plane for St. Louis that night. In the process, the meeting with the editor was forgotten until he returned to the Bay Area the following week. Hal, in the meantime, had finished writing chapter three and had started work on chapter two.

Ultimately, the miscommunication cost less than half a day's work, since most of the contents of the chapter Hal had written would be incorporated in other work. Still, the error was an irritating one, becoming the source of future anxiety about it happening again, until Hal and Dr. Gnu Etal made a pact that if either of them had a solo meeting with the editor, the editor would be responsible for supplying notes on the meeting to both collaborators within twenty-four hours.

If you are working closely with an editor, the potential for miscommunication can be eliminated by making certain that both collaborators are present at all meetings. In this respect, conference calls, that is, three-way hookups between both collaborators and the editor, can eliminate misunderstandings.

The person doing most of the writing should carry the chief responsibility for editorial meetings, making certain that his partner is filled in on editorial discussions. If one partner is left out of editorial meetings, he or she may feel neglected, even when there is no reason to feel that way. But feelings are an important element in collaborative writing, just as they are between lovers, and they should be respected.

Hal remembers how, in the beginning of his first collaboration with Mike Samuels, they were working with an editor in Berkeley, about fifty miles from Mike's home. Since Hal lived in Berkeley, only a few blocks from the editor, he and the editor met every couple of weeks, sometimes to talk about the book, sometimes just to have coffee and pass the time of day.

It was not unusual, in the course of a day's work, for Hal to talk with Mike about conversations he had with their editor. At one point Mike told Hal that he felt left out, that it seemed to him there were decisions being made that he needed to be included in. Hal assured him that he was providing Mike with feedback from the meetings with the editor, but Mike was not satisfied. Mike didn't know exactly why he felt as he did, but he did know that he wanted to be included in future editorial meetings.

Wanting to make certain the air was clear, Hal called the editor and scheduled a meeting that included all three men. That meeting went well, and Mike, Hal and the editor would try to get together for lunch at least once every two or three months. Though these meetings were not absolutely necessary—business of substance rarely being the topic of conversation—they were informative and fun. The meetings eventually became brainstorming sessions, in which the three men developed a four-book series.

Not all collaborations are quite as democratic as we've described here, nor do they have to be if that is the agreement from the start. Prentice-Hall Press's *Author's Guide*, for example, suggests that one writer be established as senior over the other. It is agreed from the start that this senior writer will be responsible for all communications and for assigning work schedules. Deciding who will be the senior writer is itself a major challenge but it must be worked out between the writers at the outset.

Sometimes, one of your team may have a better relationship with your agent or editor, so it is wise to let the person who can do it best do it. Even when there is full agreement that this should be done, it is important that the other partner be kept up to date on all decisions, and that input be heard from all participants.

Don't make the mistake of getting into power struggles over communication issues halfway through the book. If you can't find any way around it, look for a person who can act as your ombudsman, perhaps your agent or an editor or even an outside consultant with good negotiating skills. Ending a book collaboration because of an ego dispute can cost everyone money, something that few writers have a lot of. So, keep this simple rule in mind: *When it comes to a choice between ego and eating, choose eating.*

CORK-POPPING TIME

There will come a day when you and your collaborator have completed the manuscript, have incorporated voluminous editorial notes that you've both contributed, have made copies of your work, have packed it in a box and sent it off to the publisher. You go out and celebrate, content that the job is complete. All you have to do now is sit back and collect your last payment on your advance. Then the books will start appearing in the bookstores, reviews will begin to appear and by next year, the royalties will be rolling in. Right? Not quite.

Your editor will now go to work on your "finished" manuscript, and within a month or two you will receive back in the mail what was once your neatly typed manuscript. But now those crisply typed pages are marred with notes, comments, and suggested changes handwritten in the margins. What do you do now? What does all this mean? Have you failed?

Don't panic. This phase of editing is normal. Hal recalls the first manuscript he got back from his editor, with every page filled with remarks, corrections, and additions that sent his head spinning. So many thoughts and feelings are triggered at this phase of the writing. The manuscript is your creation, your baby, and you've nurtured it along for months. Up to this point you may not have felt how much a part of you it has become. You felt you had honed every sentence, shaped every chapter so that it was perfect, and now this person from the publishing house has poked holes in it that no one else would notice.

After a while, you cool down, develop a little professional detachment, and take a second look. Yes, you did leave out the reference to the quotation on page four. And, yes, as it turns out, you did spell Nietzsche's name three different ways in chapter five. And, yes, the editor just might be right that your four-page chapter on the history and importance of psychophysiological research in modern medicine probably should be expanded. You remember now that you had meant to do this before the manuscript went off in the first place. It looks to you that you just might improve the manuscript significantly by doing more work.

In *How To Write A Book Proposal,* Michael tells the following story:

> I know a writer who wanted to do a how-to book about writing because he felt it would be a great help to writers. He had a four-page brochure he had been sending out with writing instructions, and with new information he had been gathering, he felt it would add up to fifteen pages of manuscript, a good size for a little booklet.
>
> But when he revised the material, he had sixty pages of manuscript. He began working with an editor who sent him editorial suggestions. He made them and then the manuscript was eighty-seven pages. The editor then sent him nine single-spaced pages of corrections. Unhappy but persistent, he trudged on, but then found himself with a 137-page manuscript. And then came the copyediting. What was the final result of what started out to be a little booklet? You're holding it in your hands!

As Michael's story illustrates, the changes an editor suggests may lead to your decision to do a rewrite of your manuscript, or the change suggested may be minimal, limited to small organizational problems or smoothing out syntax. Regardless of how things look, as a collaborator you have a special problem that the solo writer needn't be concerned with: Who will be responsible for making the changes an editor suggests? Who will read over the editorial notes and make decisions about which ones are missing the point, and which ones indicate that either your editor is a lunatic (unlikely) or you didn't make yourself clear in the first place (hmm).

Having published more than twenty books, Hal has worked on perhaps less than a half-dozen where editors didn't request revisions. No matter how good a writer you are, having no revisions means that editors are not doing their jobs. The changes have required as little as four hours and on longer books as much as six weeks of work. On most books, the revisions have not required more than a week of work. When estimating the time for your revisions from these figures, remember that Hal is a professional writer with many books behind him.

Because revisions take time and effort, make certain you have a clause about this in your agreement with your collaborator. If the revisions are substantial, both collaborators should read them and be involved in any decisions regarding them. But as a general rule, it is important to specify in your agreement that the work of revisions will follow the same formula you worked out for writing the manuscript. If you and your collaborator have a 50-50 arrangement, then it should be noted in your agreement that you will share equally in making revisions. If you are working on a straight-fee basis, more as a ghostwriter than a collaborator, be particularly careful of defining the manner in which the revisions will be handled.

If you are the expert on the book, make certain you participate in this last phase of the project. Remember, your name will appear on the book, and you will want to make certain that everything appearing in print deserves the stamp of approval that your name implies.

Often, a flat fee means exactly that when it comes to your participation in the final editing. Let's say that you get $50,000 for writing an exercise book with a Hollywood star. Unless otherwise stated in your contract, that sum would include any rewrites your editor requires. If you want additional money for doing the revisions, or if you would like to provide a cushion for yourself should you be required to make extensive revisions, then you should include your estimate of those additional costs in your original agreement.

Whatever you do, consider revisions as an integral part of the job of writing a book and, of course, a task that should be discussed in every collaboration. And don't overlook the fact that there may be revisions of revisions.

Revisions are one thing. Copyediting is another. The latter is not as large an issue as the former. Copyediting is done by a person who specializes in catching misspellings, correcting sentence structure, and catching the thousand and one errors in fact and form that may mar a manuscript.

If you're the expert on the project, and your writer's work comes back with pages of notes and corrections, don't make the mistake of thinking that your writer is incompetent or unprofessional. There is an old joke in the publishing world:

> *First you have the writer, who can write but can't spell. Then you have the editor, who can spell but can't write. Then you have the publisher, who can neither write nor spell, and he's the one that makes all the money.*

Contrary to popular opinion, writers are not necessarily good spellers or grammarians. F. Scott Fitzgerald, for example, was an atrocious speller, and on his first novel Max Perkins, his editor, was so busy protecting the manuscript from being hacked up by copyeditors who didn't have a feeling for the novelist's style, that he forgot to check for misspellings himself. As a result, the book was published and went through five printings before all the corrections were made. Perkins, more than Fitzgerald, was deeply embarrassed by this oversight since it was the editor's, not the writer's, responsibility to see that the book was copyedited.

Copyediting does not usually require more than a few days, although we recommend that you make sure that you are given the opportunity to check the copyeditor's work, which usually takes no more than a few hours of your time.

GALLEY SLAVES

After revisions and copyediting, you have one more opportunity to look at your manuscript before it turns into a book. This final opportunity arrives in the form of the "galleys," usually long sheets of typeset material from the printer. These are the "proofs," showing how your book will look in print.

The publisher will have other people reading the proofs to check for typesetting errors. But don't depend on them to catch everything. Writers find things that proofreaders don't find, and vice versa.

You and your collaborator should plan to spend a good deal of time with the galleys. If you have any graphic materials noted by number in the text, make certain all reference numbers are correct. If you have footnotes, check them.

The galley stage is your last opportunity for making corrections. But since making changes requires work by the typesetter, beware! There may be an expense involved for you and your collaborator. You will find a clause in your contract stating that you have a certain allowance for making changes in the galleys. In most contracts, it reads something like the following, from a Random House contract:

> The Author agrees to read, revise, correct and promptly return to the Publisher all proofs of the work and to have charged against him the cost of alterations, required by the Author, other than those due to printer's errors, in excess of ten percent (10%) of the cost of setting type.

Within this clause lies an issue for potential controversy between the collaborators. Up to now the book was still a dream, something that would happen in the future. Now it is in galleys. If one is prone to such things, now is the time people get cold feet. It is a little like getting stage fright on the day you are to give a speech. When you were first asked to give the speech, three months ago, you thought it was a fine idea. You were flattered to be asked and thought it would be a snap. But now comes the day of reckoning when you have to deliver, and suddenly you're not so sure you want to do it.

Stage fright is easy for most people to understand and to sympathize with. It isn't easy getting up in front of a crowd of people to speak your mind. But hardly anyone talks about "print fright," that anxiety an author feels as his book moves toward publication and the realization that soon his words will be scrutinized by thousands of people. It may be a last ditch effort to correct syntax and rewrite paragraphs where you went out on a limb further than you should have, or as a sudden realization that the book absolutely must be reorganized. The fact that no one else noticed these things until now is peculiar. In fact, that's usually how you diagnose this disease we call print fright: When there are changes that simply must be made that no one but you has previously spotted and which no one but you, even now, can see any reason for. That these changes have slipped past everyone suggests that the need for them may exist mostly in your mind. If you recognize these symptoms in yourself at this point, there is one cure for it: Tell yourself it is time to let go.

If there is only one author to deal with, there is little room for controversy. The changes can be made and the author will have to foot the bill for any changes over the allowance. However, if you're a coauthor working on a 50-50 split and you can't see the reason for $700 worth of last-minute changes ordered by your partner, you may be in for a fight. That's the best reason in the world to make certain that you spell out your responsibilities in your original working agreement, or preferably in your contract with the publisher. One simple criterion for doing this is to have it in writing that both authors must agree to all galley changes.

Hal recalls one project in which his collaborator, a psychotherapist, made $1,200 worth of author's changes on the galleys. In looking over these changes, Hal could only justify about a tenth of them. The rest of the changes were a matter of taste, breaking a longer paragraph into two, italicizing words for emphasis that were not originally italicized. In one chapter the order of ten paragraphs had been altered. Although he could recognize the reasons for the changes, he did not feel the changes were warranted, or that many readers or editors would ever notice the necessity for such changes.

An argument ensued between the writers, and eventually the changes were negotiated. Hal agreed that half the changes made at least some improvement in the book, the others were only a whim. He ended up paying for a little over a third of the changes, with his partner agreeing to pay for the other two-thirds, to be deducted accordingly from his royalties.

Though in Hal's case an equitable agreement was negotiated, the episode illustrates the problems that can arise even after the manuscript is finished.

MARKETING

Although not true with every book, marketing is essentially a team project, and all parties involved in the writing, even though they may not take an active role in promotion, should be present at marketing discussions. Without that, the absent celebrity or collaborator may feel that sales would have been better had he been present to add his two cents' worth to the marketing and promotion plan.

There are two kinds of marketing: 1) selling the proposal of the book to a publisher; and 2) promoting the book to the book-buying public.

In the case of selling the proposal, the collaborators usually should take equally active roles during any contacts they have with editors or agents who show an interest in the project. When this is not feasible, the partner who takes responsibility for such meetings should immediately get back to the other with a full report of what transpired.

In most cases, editors and agents want to know exactly whom they're dealing with. They know that collaborations are not always easy, and to see the collaborators together helps to give the publisher a feeling for the writers' relationship. When one of the collaborators is a celebrity, that person may do a better job of selling the book when the collaborator is tagging along.

Book promotion brings up similar issues. When it comes to the promotion of collaboration, several possibilities exist: First, on projects with an expert or celebrity, it is common for that person to make public appearances alone. It is, after all, their expertise or public recognition that sells the book. But even in this there are exceptions. In the medical books Hal wrote with Mike Samuels, Mike, being the doctor, was clearly the one with expertise in the medical field. But the books they did together were written specifically for the general public, and that is where Hal came in. His expertise in translating difficult medical concepts into lay terms was an important contribution. Over the years, Mike and Hal have done several promotion tours together, with Hal taking an *expert role* as a lay person able to deal with medical concepts previously thought to be the exclusive property of the doctor. That role helped sell their books, since it proved that lay people were capable of taking responsibility in medical decisions that affected them—and that, of course, was important in their books.

At other times, however, Hal took a back seat while his co-author did the publicity tours alone. This was the case with John Marino, whose world-record-breaking transcontinental bike ride won him instant access to national media; with Charles Garfield, who had already established himself as one of the most sought-after speakers on the national lecture circuit: and with others whose reputations preceded the publication of their books.

Marketing and promotion questions should, of course, be negotiated early in the project. Who does the publicity for the book will also affect how the names are listed on the cover. For example, if there is an expert who will be doing the publicity, it is wise to give that person credit as the main author, with his or her name listed in large letters and "with" So-and-so, his collaborator, listed in smaller letters under his. This saves the person doing the publicity many moments of embarrassed silence when a television interviewer asks him, on the air, where the "other author" is. Listing one name over another in such cases also helps keep the focus on the expert, and usually makes it easier for the public to remember the name when they order the book.

PROMOTIONAL CONSIDERATIONS

Promotion of a book can be even more important than content. A man once wrote to Michael with an outline for an extremely promotable book. While the manuscript itself was poorly written, the author himself was highly promotable. Being a PR man himself, he had excellent contacts with the media.

Michael urged the writer to develop the material, so that he would have a book that would warrant the publicity he would put into it. His efforts backfired. The author went to another agent and, on the basis of his promotional abilities he got a large advance from a publisher who didn't care how well the book was written.

Publicity is a tremendously important part of the package you are selling to a publisher. If you can put together a plan to promote the book, and you have media contacts who will make it possible to get television and radio exposure, you're almost assured of a contract.

If you can put together a publicity plan, along with a manuscript that delivers what it says it will—and which appeals to readers in a way that will encourage them to recommend your book to their friends and associates—you have a winning combination. By far the most appealing promotional plan, from the publisher's point of view, is the one that authors can do on their own, independent of the publisher. A publisher's dream: a nationally recognized speaker or public figure with an appealing, well-written book who is a close personal friend of Johnny Carson, Phil Donahue, and Oprah Winfrey.

SUMMARY: A NEW GROUND BREAKING

In today's publishing world, collaborative writing has evolved into an art form in itself, a kind of writing that is quite different from the ghostwriting tradition of even a decade ago. From seeking out collaborators, to defining the working relationship, through writing, revisions, and publicity, the new collaborators are much more than writers providing services for people who can't or don't want to write.

The experiences of the new collaborators reveal that the total benefits of collaboration are larger than the sum of its parts. In an especially dynamic coauthorship, the finished manuscript will be richer than either of the writers could have produced alone.

In many successful collaborations, such as those of Lawrence and Lee, and Epps and Cash, the writers report the experience of creating a third "voice," a writing voice or mind that is different from either of the writers creating it. It is as though the collaborators have created a super character, one who is not a character in their book but a silent partner in the process of the writing itself. When this occurs, it is one of the most exciting and rewarding writing experiences one can have.

Of course, not every collaboration works this way. For many collaborative writers, the working arrangement is divided between research and writing, with one person doing the former, the other the latter. But even in the most down-to-earth collaborations there are benefits that one cannot enjoy when writing alone.

We have tried to describe a number of collaborative arrangements, so that you and your collaborator may find the writing relationship that works best for you both. We've discussed how collaborative writing might be compared to a marriage or a love affair, in which there must be a balance between creative autonomy and cooperation, a balance that often evolves as harmony in any intimate relationship. Luck and personal chemistry account for much in collaborative writing but there are skills you can develop to make that chemistry work.

Our intention has been not simply to create rules for the right and wrong ways to collaborate but to provide guidelines for making choices and tailoring a collaboration that will work well for you and your cowriter. Our goal is to provide you not so much with all the answers but, more importantly, with the right questions that will produce the answers you need to bring out the full talents of your writing team.

Writers know that the creation of a book is a special act: The best books, coming from the heart, are products of love or represent major investments of one's personal resources. These creations are also special because they entertain, enlighten, or give comfort to thousands or even millions of people. In this respect, the working relationship out of which a book, especially a collaboration, is produced can be critical.

We can describe the basic ingredients that one needs to make a collaboration work well, but mixing those ingredients and adding your own special style, skill, and creativity is the final act that will give your project its own special touch of magic. It was Max Perkins who said, "A writer's best work comes entirely from himself." The collaborations that are possible in today's publishing world give new meaning to Perkins' statement, with the merging of two or more minds, each contributing his or her best work to the creation of a single book.

Books, like close friendships and harmonious marriages are the products of love, the willingness to translate the best in oneself into an expression that the rest of the world can enjoy. Those collaborations that have truly succeeded, artistically, commercially, or both, have been rare combinations of committed friendship, craft, and hard work. It is the kind of work that transforms the workaday world into sheer joy. How better then to close this book than with the words of Kahlil Gibran:

> *"Work is love made visible. And if you cannot work with love . . . it is better that you should leave your work and sit at the gate of the temple and take alms of those who work with joy."*

APPENDIX A

Sample: Collaboration Agreement

The following collaboration agreement, prepared by an author's literary attorney, is but one way to prepare such a document. It is presented here as a sample only. We recommend that you use this only as a rough model; since every collaboration is unique, each should be approached in a way that will define the special rights, risks, and responsibilities of the participants.

COLLABORATION AGREEMENT

Authors' agreement made this day, June 31, 1988, between Joe D. Authority, and Jane Rittenbook:

Joe D. Authority desires at his expense and under his direction to retain and commission Jane Rittenbook to assist in preparing a proposal for, and then a full manuscript of, a trade book entitled *Peaceful Work Places,* containing a system of conflict resolution for corporate managers, and which is the subject of a seminar program owned by Nice Guys Systems, Inc.

In consideration of the mutual covenants contained herein, it is agreed as follows:

1. *WARRANTIES AND REPRESENTATIONS OF* Joe D. Authority: Joe D. Authority warrants and represents that he has the right to enter into this agreement, and that he has no outstanding commitments or contracts that will interfere with his performance of this agreement.

138

2. *WARRANTIES AND REPRESENTATIONS OF* Jane Rittenbook: Jane Rittenbook warrants and represents that she has the right to enter into this agreement, and that she has no outstanding commitments or contracts that will interfere with her performance of this agreement.

3. *MATERIALS TO BE FURNISHED BY* Joe D. Authority: Joe D. Authority shall make available to Jane Rittenbook materials from the Nice Guys System, Inc., training programs, to help in the preparation of the proposal and manuscript described in paragraphs 5 and 6. Joe D. Authority shall also make available interviews with his training staff, and give Jane Rittenbook access to seminars at no cost, which are pertinent to the development of the proposal and manuscript.

4. *JANE RITTENBOOK'S SERVICES:* Jane Rittenbook will provide Joe D. Authority her writing services for the purpose of preparing the proposal and manuscript, as described in paragraphs 5 and 6 below.

5. *THE PROPOSAL:* Jane Rittenbook shall prepare a proposal for the Work.

The proposal shall consist of the following elements: (a) Overview of the book's contents, market potential, special markets, estimated length in manuscript pages, date of completion, and the credentials and credits of the authors; (b) a detailed table of contents, and working chapter outline; and (c) sample text to consist of two chapters.

The proposal will be considered complete when it is satisfactory to Joe D. Authority and his agent, Page Sellers, who will be handling the Work, who together will judge its readiness for submission to publishers.

Jane Rittenbook shall begin work on the proposal no later than June 31, 1988, and shall complete this proposal no later than forty-five days from that date.

6. *THE MANUSCRIPT:* At such time that a publisher has entered into an agreement to publish the Work, Joe D. Authority shall begin writing the complete manuscript, with the assistance of Jane Rittenbook, based on the proposal as described herein.

Jane Rittenbook shall prepare the manuscript in a professional manner, and both authors will work together in accordance with a schedule that will permit the completion of the Work in a form acceptable to the Publisher, in accordance with any contract with the same.

7. *AUTHORS' CREDITS:* Authors' credits on the finished book will be accorded as "By Joe D. Authority, with Jane Rittenbook." The name of the first author listed, Joe D. Authority, shall appear in larger type than the second, Jane Rittenbook. All public appearances, television interviews, or other interviews regarding the book, will be conducted by Joe D. Authority.

8. *AGENCY REPRESENTATION:* Page Sellers, 101 Fifth Avenue, New York, New York is hereby appointed as the exclusive agent for the purpose of negotiating contracts arising from this agreement, at a commission of fifteen percent (15%) of all monies derived from contracts made by this agency.

All payments to the authors, arising out of the Work herein described, and represented by Page Sellers, will be made to and in the name of Page Sellers, and that agent will remit payments to all parties as provided in paragraph 9.

9. *PAYMENTS:*
A. Joe D. Authority shall pay Jane Rittenbook the following sums for the preparation of the proposal:
  1. Upon signing of this agreement: $2500.
  2. Forty-five days following $1250.
  3. Upon completion of the proposal: $1250.
B. In connection with Jane Rittenbook's completion of the Manuscript, Joe D. Authority shall remit to Jane Rittenbook forty percent (40%) of all receipts from the publication of the Work, after the deduction from such receipts of the following: (a) agency commissions to Page Sellers, as provided in paragraph 8; (b) all expenses and payments agreed upon by both authors in connection with the publication of the book, such as index, photos, and the preparation of this contract, provided that from the remaining receipts Jane Rittenbook shall first receive $30,000 or forty percent (40%) of any advance payments provided under

the terms agreed upon with the publisher.

C. Notwithstanding the foregoing, and in the event that the remaining receipts from advance payments would amount to less than $30,000, either party shall have the right to terminate this agreement, upon written notice to the other within ten (10) days after notification of advance payment terms by the proposed agreement between the publisher and the authors. In the event of such termination, Jane Rittenbook shall return all materials to Joe. D. Authority and the proposal shall become his property only. Jane Rittenbook shall have no rights, obligations, or liabilities to the Work, or to this agreement thereafter.

10. *PROJECT EXPENSES:* All reasonable expenses incurred by the authors in connection with the Work, including but not limited to travel, communication, research, and secretarial expenses, shall be divided equally between the two authors, pursuant to the publication agreement described herein. In the case of single expenditures over $250, such expenditures must be discussed and agreed upon by both authors prior to being incurred.

11. *COPYRIGHTS:* The authors will jointly own all rights, titles and interests in the book itself, but Joe D. Authority will have sole right and ownership of all electronic, film, and other media forms, as well as workshops, that are derived from this work. Jane Rittenbook hereby assigns to Joe D. Authority all rights to the work except those pertaining directly to the sale of the book itself.

12. *ASSIGNMENT:* Neither author will assign or transfer its obligations or rights under this agreement, except for its rights to receive monies, without the prior written consent and agreement of the other. Any violation will render such assignments null and void.

13. *WARRANTIES AND INDEMNIFICATIONS:* Each party represents, warrants, and agrees that the material written or otherwise contributed by it is wholly original and will not violate or conflict with the rights of any other person, firm, or corporation. Each party agrees to indemnify and hold the other harmless against any claims, demands, suits, costs, losses, damages or recoveries (including amounts paid in settlement or in reasonable attorney's fees), by reason of its breach of any of the warranties or representations contained herein.

14. *ARBITRATION:* Any controversy arising out of this agreement will be settled by arbitration in New York City in accordance with the rules of the American Arbitration Association, and judgment upon the award rendered may be entered in any court having jurisdiction.

15. *TERMS:* The term of this agreement shall be coextensive with the period of the longest term of copyright, anywhere in the world, in the Work.

16. *FURTHER ASSURANCES:* The parties agree to execute any other agreements, execute any other documents, and take any other steps that may be necessary or convenient to carry out the terms and intent of this agreement.

17. *NOTICE:* All notices given under the terms of this agreement shall be in writing and shall be sent by certified mail, return receipt requested, addressed to the authors at their respective addresses, with a copy to the agent representing them, who is: Page Sellers.

18. *NO PARTNERSHIP:* Nothing contained in this agreement shall in any way be construed to imply or create a partnership or joint venture relationship between the authors, or to constitute one author as the agent for the other.

19. *BINDING AGREEMENT:* This agreement shall enure to the benefit of and be binding upon the executors, administrators, and permitted assigns of the authors.

20. *GOVERNING LAW:* This agreement shall be construed and enforced in accordance with the internal laws of the State of New York applicable to agreements entered into and performed entirely in that State.

21. *HEADINGS:* The headings contained in this agreement are for convenience only, and they shall not affect the interpretation of the provisions described.

22. *ENTIRE AGREEMENT:* This agreement constitutes the total understanding between the parties, and it cannot be changed or terminated except by written instrument executed by all parties herein named.

APPROVED:

(Joe D. Authority) (Date)

(Jane Rittenbook) (Date)

(Page Sellers, literary agent) (Date)

Note: There is no intent, on the part of the authors or publisher to provide this instrument as a legal document. This contract is presented here as a rough sample only. It is not intended to be used in place of a legal document drawn up for collaborators by a qualified attorney, nor should readers take this as a full or partial legal representation of any written agreement they might make with their coauthor.

APPENDIX B

Sample: Ghostwriter's Working Agreement

A statement of intent or working agreement is as important for the ghostwriter as it is for the collaborator. The following is an example of one ghostwriter's agreement with his collaborator, written in the form of a letter.

Dear Max Doe:

RE: Statement of Intent/Ghostwriter

This is a letter of intent, spelling out an agreement for our work together on your book *The Scarlet Pickle,* a detective novel.

It is my understanding that you want me to work with you as a ghostwriter. I understand this means the following:

1. I will work as a contractor, and on an hourly rate, that being $35 per hour, with the addition of bonuses as described in #8 below.

2. I will follow your lead where ideas and story research for the book are concerned. I will, however, participate in this process in a creative and cooperative manner, contributing both my writing skills and my ideas in the way to which we have become accustomed in our work together these past few weeks.

3. The first part of our work together will be to produce two sample chapters, to be sent to your agent for his feedback and approval. We will also produce a chapter outline that will provide us with a "map" through the book. Should your agent ask for revisions of the written material, I will make them at your request, and at the agreed-upon rate for my time.

4. I understand that I am not a coauthor, meaning that I will not share in royalties you may earn in the future, and you will be recognized as the sole author of the work.

5. After the proposal is completed, I understand that you will want to proceed with the writing, again on a continuing contract basis, paying me the same rate as stated above, in addition to bonuses described in #8, below.

6. I understand that in signing this statement of intent I will commit myself, insofar as is possible, to the completion of the project with you, unless we decide mutually to dissolve our working relationship.

7. If a dissolution of the working relationship should become necessary or desired by one or both of us, it will be done as follows: First, we will put the reason for the dissolution in writing and present it to the other person. If personal conflicts are involved in this decision, we will make every effort to work them out, including calling in a third party (not to exceed three hours of consulting time, any costs to be equally shared) to help resolve the issues. Should dissolution be agreed upon by both of us, we will put that fact in writing, releasing us both from any obligations spelled out or implied in this letter.

8. Bonuses: If the book should sell over 100,000 copies, I will receive a bonus of $10,000, in addition to the above contract agreement. If the book sells over 300,000 copies, I will receive, in addition to money already received, the sum of $25,000. If the book sells over a million copies, I will receive an additional $30,000. This will be spelled out in a rider on the book contract that you receive from the publisher, and payment will be made to me through your agent.

9. I understand that the main ideas for this book, namely the story line and plot that you have developed, and the characters that you have outlined, are your property, and I will do nothing to infringe on these rights. I will not write books or articles using these ideas, that might compete with your work, for two years.

10. We will set up regular meeting times of approximately four hours per week to work on the book together. I will be paid at the agreed-upon rate for these meetings. Outside the meetings we will both work alone on the book.

11. You will pay me an advance of $750 against the first month's pay, to start the work, said sum applied against work as it is completed. I will keep an accurate accounting of my hours, and submit to you a bill on the first of each month, to be paid by the fifth.

12. We will make every effort to complete the sample chapters and outline within forty-five days of the signing of this agreement. The total time I spend in writing the sample chapters and outline should not exceed 100 hours. I will let you know of any changes in that estimate should it become necessary, or should it be required because of changes you wish to make.

I understand that this is simply a statement of intent, and that it does not replace personal trust and good faith established by our actions.

_____

(Ghostwriter's Signature)   *Date*

_____

(Author's Signature)   *Date*

Note: This document is presented only to give writers a broad picture of the general content of such an instrument. It is not intended as, and should not be used as, a model for a legal document.

APPENDIX C

Michael Larsen's Collaboration Agreement

Below is the basic collaboration agreement that Michael Larsen uses when he represents both collaborators on a 50/50 deal for a nonfiction book. If it is successful, a collaboration represented by Michael's agency involves at least four agreements. First, both authors sign copies of Michael's agency agreement (which is included in Appendix D.) This agency agreement covers issues that would otherwise be addressed in some collaboration agreements. Having signed that agreement, the collaborators prepare a proposal "on spec" and without compensation.

After producing the proposal, the authors sign the following agreement, which puts in writing the terms that they agreed on before they began working on the proposal. The agreement usually requires modification to meet the needs of particular collaborators. Despite its clarity, informality, and California tone, the agreement is valid.

When the proposal sells, the collaborators commit themselves to the more comprehensive legal, literary, and financial terms of the publisher's contract.

COLLABORATORS' AGREEMENT

In the spirit of trust and good faith, we, Harriet Ormsby Fortesquieu and Wright Eweare, agree to collaborate on a book now called *Sleepwalking for Fun and Profit*.

Harriet will provide the information. Wright will be responsible for writing the book.

All references to the book's authorship will read: "by Harriet Ormsby Fortesquieu and Wright Eweare." Copyright will al-

147

ways be secured in both names. Both of us must sign all agreements relating to the book.

We will share the expenses of writing the book equally. All expenses of more than $50 will be agreed upon in advance.

All proceeds from all present and future rights to the book in all forms and media throughout the world, less literary agency commissions and expenses, will be divided equally between us. The division of the proceeds will apply to our respective heirs and assigns.

Both of our signatures are needed to change this agreement, which is not the basis of a partnership, and which will be interpreted according to California law.

Both of us are represented by Michael Larsen/Elizabeth Pomada Literary Agents, who agree to settle disputes arising from this agreement with fairness to both of us. We agree to settle disputes Michael and Elizabeth can't resolve with a mediator or arbitrator we both agree on. Each of us and the agency has a copy of this agreement.

_____

(Harriet Ormsby Fortesquieu)   *Date*

_____

(Wright Eweare)   *Date*

APPENDIX D

Sample: Agent's Contract

Dear Michael and Elizabeth:

While trust, friendliness, and confidence are the basis for our relationship, I have read your brochure, and I am ready to put our commitments to each other in writing.

I appoint you my sole agent to advise me and negotiate sales of all kinds for books I ask you to represent me on and their subsidiary rights in all forms and media and for all future uses throughout the world. You may appoint co-agents to help you.

If an idea is mine and we do not develop it together, only I have the rights to the idea or any basic variation on it. However, if another writer approaches you with the same idea or a similar idea, you are free to represent the project. If the idea for a project is yours, only you have the rights to the idea or any basic variation on it. You may represent a project competitive to mine, provided that in your judgment, it doesn't lessen your ability to represent my work.

You will pay for all expenses which arise in selling my work except photocopying my work and mailing it abroad or on multiple submissions; buying galleys and books; and legal advice. I must approve in advance all expenses over $50 for which I will be responsible.

You may receive on my behalf all money due me from agreements signed through your efforts. This includes all sales for which negotiations begin during the term of this agreement and end within six months after it expires, and all changes and extensions in those agreements, regardless of when made, or by whom.

You are irrevocably entitled to deduct 15% commission on all gross income negotiated on my behalf, including production costs, earned through your agency. For foreign rights, you may deduct 20%, which includes 10% for your co-agents. All commissions you receive will not be returnable for any reason.

I must first approve all offers and then sign all agreements negotiated on my behalf. Michael Larsen/Elizabeth Pomada Literary Agents will be named as my agency in all agreements I sign on all projects represented by you.

You will remit all money and statements due me within 10 working days of receiving them.

You may respond to mail received on my behalf unless it is personal, in which case you will forward it to me promptly. I will notify you promptly if I change my phone number or address.

I realize it may take years to sell a project and you agree to try as long as you believe it is possible. You will notify me promptly when you think a project is no longer salable, and then I may do with it as I wish without obligation to you.

If a problem arises about your efforts or our relationship, I will contact you and we will conscientiously try to solve the problem with fairness to both of us. A problem we can't settle will be resolved with an arbitrator you and I choose.

You or I may end this agreement with 60 days notice by registered mail. However, you will be entitled to receive statements and commissions on all rights on properties on which you make the initial sale, whether or not the agency represents me on the sales of these rights.

This agreement is binding on our respective personal and business heirs and assigns and will be interpreted according to California law.

I am free to sign this agreement and will not agree to a conflicting obligation. I will sign two copies of this agreement and each of us will have one. Both of our signatures are needed to change this agreement.

Like you, I am signing this agreement in the hope that it will symbolize our mutual long-term commitment to the development of my career and to sharing the satisfaction and rewards of this growth.

Date: _____

_____
My Signature

_____
For Michael Larsen/
Elizabeth Pomada

_____
My Name Printed

_____
Birthdate

_____
Address

_____
Social Security Number

_____
Home Phone

_____
How I was referred to you

_____
Office Phone

APPENDIX E

Publisher's Contract

Writer's Digest Books / North Light Books

F&W Publications, Inc.
1507 Dana Avenue
Cincinnati, Ohio 45207

AGREEMENT

THIS AGREEMENT dated the   , between
F&W Publications, Inc., dba Writer's Digest Books/North Light Books, 1507 Dana Avenue,
Cincinnati, Ohio 45207 (hereinafter referred to as "Publisher") and

(hereinafter referred to as "Author," and by the masculine singular pronoun), whose address is:

1. EXCLUSIVE PUBLISHING RIGHT

The Author hereby grants to the Publisher the exclusive right to produce in book form, and sell directly or through others ("publish"), a work to be prepared by the Author now tentatively titled

(hereinafter referred to as "the Work"). The Author also hereby grants to the Publisher the right to produce and sell, and to permit others to produce and sell, reprint and book club editions, adaptations, abridgments, condensations, and selections from the Work, motion pictures, radio and television broadcasts, or recordings based on the Work, novelty or commercial use of the Work, and use of the Work in any means of storage, retrieval, dissemination, and reproduction of information (the "subsidiary rights"). Publisher's right to publish, and the subsidiary rights herein granted, shall be exclusive worldwide in all languages.

2. COMPETING WORKS

While this Agreement is in effect, the Author shall not, without the prior written consent of the Publisher, write, edit, or publish, or cause to be written, edited, or published, any other work or any other edition of the Work, whether revised, enlarged, abridged, or otherwise, that might interfere with or injure the sales of the Work or any grant of rights or licenses by the Publisher permitted under this Agreement, nor shall the Author permit the use of his name or likeness in connection with any such work.

3. AUTHOR'S WARRANTIES

The Author warrants and represents to the Publisher that:

(a) the Author is the sole and exclusive owner of the rights herein granted to the Publisher;

(b) the Work has not heretofore been published, except as follows:

(c) the Author has not heretofore assigned, pledged, or otherwise encumbered the rights herein granted to the Publisher;

(d) the Work violates no copyright, either in whole or in part, and the Author will obtain and forward to the Publisher all necessary permissions and licenses for the use of copyrighted text or illustrations contained in the Work, for all editions and uses of the Work throughout the world;

(e) the Work is not in the public domain;

(f) the Work contains no matter which would be libelous or defamatory, or infringe any trade name or trademark, or invade any right of privacy or proprietary right, and it contains no injurious formulas or instructions;

(g) all statements of fact contained in the Work are true or based upon reasonable research;

The foregoing warranties and representations shall survive any termination of this Agreement, and at all times the Author shall, at his expense, indemnify and defend the Publisher, and hold the Publisher and its licensees harmless against any claim, loss, or liability sustained by reason of a breach of any of the foregoing warranties and representations. The Publisher shall promptly notify the Author of any claim or suit which may involve any of the foregoing warranties and representations, and the Author will cooperate fully in the defense thereof; provided, however, the Publisher and its attorney shall have the right to control the defense, or with the Author's consent, the settlement thereof. The Author shall, in all events, be entitled to employ his own attorney, who shall cooperate with the Publisher's attorney in all proceedings hereinunder.

If such claim or suit is not finally sustained, the Publisher shall bear one-half of the counsel fees and other costs incurred, except where the Author, prior to publication, had refused to revise the manuscript in connection with such matter at the Publisher's request.

Without limiting any other remedies which the Publisher may have, any payments that would otherwise be due the Author under Paragraph 11 may be offset by any liability or expense the Publisher may incur as a result of a breach of the foregoing warranties and representations.

These warranties do not apply to any material inserted in the Work by the Publisher.

4. MANUSCRIPT

(a) The Author shall deliver to the Publisher not later than
two complete copies (the original and a duplicate) of the typewritten or printed out manuscript of the Work, which shall contain approximately   words and be
acceptable in form, style, and content to the Publisher, and the Author shall retain a third copy of the manuscript. Whether the manuscript is typewritten or printed out, it shall be double-spaced, clean, and readily legible, and if printed out, it shall be provided in separate pages, not a single continuous printout sheet.

The Author will supply with the manuscript all necessary releases, licenses, and permissions for copyrighted material contained in the Work; table of contents, preface, foreword, if any; bibliography or glossary, if any; and the following illustrations, together with all captions they require:

If the Author shall fail to do so, the Publisher shall have the right to supply said illustrations and charge the cost thereof against any sums that may accrue to the Author under the terms of this Agreement.

Time is of the essence in the Author's obligation to deliver an acceptable manuscript, and if delivery is not made on or before the stipulated date, the Publisher may, at its option at any time after sixty (60) days following such date, terminate this Agreement by notice to the Author.

The Publisher shall, within ninety (90) days from the date of its receipt thereof, accept the manuscript or return it for correction or revision. In the event that the Publisher returns the manuscript to the Author for correction or revision, the Author shall make such corrections or revisions within the time and in the substantive form and editorial style required by the Publisher, and the Publisher shall have the right, upon the Author's failure or refusal to do so, to terminate this Agreement by notice to the Author.

(b) Upon such termination, the Author shall return to the Publisher all amounts theretofore advanced by the Publisher to the Author on account of the Work, and upon such repayment, the Publisher shall reassign to the Author all rights granted to the Publisher under this Agreement.

(c) In the event that the Author shall become unable to carry out his responsibilities under this Agreement or shall die at any time before completion of the Work or of all revisions deemed necessary and desirable by the Publisher, the Author or the Author's representative shall appoint an appropriate person, acceptable to the Publisher, to complete the Work and/or all necessary revisions. In the event that the Author or the Author's representative declines to designate someone to perform these functions, the Publisher shall have the right to do so, and all fees or costs incurred in the completion and/or revision of the Work by the designated person shall be charged against the amounts otherwise accruing to the Author under this Agreement.

5. CORRECTION OF PROOFS

The Author shall have the right to review the copyedited manuscript, and the Publisher shall provide the Author with proofs of the Work. The Author shall return such proofs to the Publisher with corrections noted within   days after receipt thereof by the Author. If the Author fails to return such corrected proofs within such period, the Publisher may publish the Work without the Author's corrections. Any cost of alterations in type or in film required by the Author, other than those due to printer's or Publisher's error, in excess of ten percent (10%) of the original cost of composition shall be charged against payments otherwise due Author under Paragraph 11; provided, however, that upon the Author's request, the Publisher shall furnish to the Author an itemized statement of such additional expenses, and provide the Author with the corrected proofs for his inspection.

6. INDEXING

The Author shall prepare an index for the Work, and shall deliver such index to the Publisher not later than   days after the Author receives page proofs of the Work. If the Author so desires, the Publisher will engage the services of others to do an index for the Work, and the cost of this service shall be charged against payments otherwise due Author under Paragraph 11.

7. PUBLICATION

The Publisher will publish the Work at its expense, except as otherwise provided herein, within eighteen (18) months after acceptance by Publisher of the completed, acceptable manuscript as required under Paragraph 4. In the event Publisher is prevented from publishing the Work within such time for extraordinary causes beyond its control, the publication date shall be extended for the amount of time during which Publisher was so prevented from publishing.

The Publisher shall have the right to publish the Work in such form as it deems best suited to the sale of the Work; to fix or alter the prices at which the Work shall be sold; and to determine the methods and means of advertising, publicizing, and selling the Work, the number and destination of free copies, and all other publishing details. All of the Publisher's decisions about format, design, editorial style, and production specifications shall be final.

The Publisher may use the Author's name and likeness or photograph in connection with the advertising and promotion of the Work, and the Author will make himself available, upon the Publisher's request, to publicize and promote the Work.

8. COPYRIGHT

The Author owns the copyright in the Work. The Publisher will print the Author's name as the copyright owner on the copyright page of every copy of the Work, in the correct form to comply with the U.S. Copyright Act and the Universal Copyright Convention. Within three (3) months of first publication, the Publisher will register the Author's name as "claimant" with the United States Copyright Office. Any license granted by the Publisher to a third party to reproduce and distribute copies of the Work will require the licensee to print the appropriate copyright notice in the Author's name in all copies, and the Publisher shall make any additional registrations or applications necessary to protect the Author's copyright in any subsidiary uses of the Work.

If any registered copyright therein shall be in the name of any person or party other than the Author, the Author shall deliver to the Publisher legally recordable assignment or assignments of such copyright or copyrights before the book goes to press.

If the Publisher considers it appropriate to manufacture the Work abroad and import more than fifteen hundred (1500) copies into the United States, it reserves the right to do so and thus waive the United States copyright as required by law.

If this Agreement has not by then been terminated, the Publisher shall apply for any necessary renewal or extension of the copyright in the Author's name.

9. INFRINGEMENT

If either party desires to make a claim for infringement of the copyright in the Work or other unauthorized use of the Work by another, such party shall notify the other party of such claim prior to or as promptly after asserting such claims as is reasonably possible. Publisher and Author shall have the right to prosecute jointly any claim for infringement or unauthorized use, provided that the party notified of such claim shall within ten (10) days of such notification notify the other party of its intention to proceed jointly. If the parties proceed jointly, the expenses and recovery, if any, shall be shared equally. If either party refuses to proceed jointly, the other party shall have the right to proceed alone and shall bear all expenses thereof and shall be exclusively entitled to any recovery, and if the Author refuses to so proceed, the Publisher may assert such claim or file suit in the Author's name.

10. REVISION AND UPDATING

The Author shall, upon the Publisher's request, revise or update the Work from time to time after publication to keep the material current. Should the Author be unable or unwilling to perform such revision, or should the Author be deceased, the revision shall be performed by the revisor designated by the Author. If the revisor or revisors designated by the Author are unable to perform such revision, or if the Author has not designated a revisor, it shall be performed by a revisor chosen by the Publisher in consultation with the Author's personal representative. Any compensation paid by the Publisher or expenses incurred in connection therewith shall be charged against payments otherwise due the Author under Paragraph 11, and the Publisher may display in the revised Work, and in advertising, the name of the person or persons who revised the Work.

If the revision is of a nature and scale as to require extensive rewriting and retypesetting, and the Publisher plans to republish and promote the Work as a revised edition, an advance proportionate to the extent of the necessary revision will be negotiated, and the provisions of this Agreement shall otherwise apply to such revision as though that revision were the Work being published for the first time.

11. ROYALTIES AND OTHER PAYMENTS TO AUTHOR

The Publisher shall pay to the Author the following advances, royalties, and payments:

ADVANCE

(a) An advance against all monies first accruing to the Author under this Agreement, of
payable as follows:

upon receipt by the Publisher of a copy of this Agreement signed by the Author;

upon receipt of the complete and final manuscript acceptable to the Publisher, together with all necessary permissions, illustrations, and captions; and

upon the Publisher's receipt of the corrected proofs from the Author.

ROYALTIES ON THE SALE OF COPIES

(b) On sales of any hardcover edition of the Work published by the Publisher and sold in the United States through normal book trade retail and wholesale channels, a royalty of:

ten percent (10%) on copies 1–10,000

twelve and one-half percent (12½%) on copies 10,001–20,000

fifteen percent (15%) on copies 20,001–30,000, and

twenty percent (20%) on all copies sold thereafter

based on Publisher's net receipts. As used in Paragraph 11(b) of this Agreement, net receipts means Publisher's list price less distributor's or bookseller's discount, returns, and credits.

(c) On sales of any paperback edition of the Work published by the Publisher and sold in the United States through normal book trade retail and wholesale channels, a royalty of:

ten percent (10%) on copies 1–20,000

twelve and one-half percent (12½%) on copies 20,001–40,000, and

fifteen percent (15%) on all copies sold thereafter

based on Publisher's net receipts. As used in Paragraph 11(c) of this Agreement, net receipts means Publisher's list price less distributor's or bookseller's discount, returns, and credits.

(d) On copies or sets of unbound sheets of the United States edition sold in Canada or anywhere in the world other than the United States and its territories and dependencies: one-half of the royalty specified in 11(b) and (c) above.

(e) On copies of the Work sold by the Publisher direct to consumers, a royalty of ten percent (10%) of Publisher's net receipts.

(f) On copies of the Work used as textbooks or premiums in the Publisher's own correspondence courses, a royalty of three percent (3%) of Publisher's list price.

(g) Should the Publisher find itself with an overstock of the Work on hand when, in its sole judgment, the demand for the Work would not use up the stock within two (2) years, it shall have the right to sell such copies at the best price it can secure. The Author shall have first option to buy any such overstock, in minimum quantities of 25 copies, at the best price obtainable from any third party. If such overstock is sold at a price below manufacturing cost, no royalty shall be paid on copies thus sold. If sold at a price above the manufacturing cost, but at a discount of seventy percent (70%) or more, the Author shall receive a royalty of ten percent (10%) of net receipts, except that the Author's royalty shall not reduce the Publisher's net receipts below the manufacturing cost. No overstock sale of copies of the Work shall occur prior to one (1) year from the date of first publication hereunder, nor shall any such sale be construed as declaring the Work either "out of print" or "off sale" in regular distribution.

(h) If the Publisher finds it necessary to remainder its entire stock or the remaining copies of an edition which has become obsolete and is being replaced by a revised edition: If the remainder selling price is less than the manufacturing expense, no royalty will be paid the Author. However, if the remainder selling price exceeds manufacturing expense, the Publisher will pay the Author ten percent (10%) of the actual cash received over manufacturing expense, for such a sale. No remainder sale may take place before one (1) year from the date of first publication of the Work in book form, and Author shall have first option to purchase "remainder copies" of the Work at the best price obtainable from any third party, or the cost of manufacture, if there is no such offer.

ROYALTIES ON THE SUBSIDIARY RIGHTS

(i) On a license of the right to another to publish a paperback or hardcover edition of the Work, fifty percent (50%) of Publisher's receipts.

(j) On a license to book clubs to produce the Work, either in whole or in condensation, and distribute it to their members: fifty percent (50%) of the monies received by the Publisher, whether as royalty or otherwise.

(k) On copies of the Work sold to the Publisher's own or other book clubs as main or alternate selections, a royalty of five percent (5%) of Member's Price. On books used as new-member inducements or bonus books in any of the Publisher's own or other book clubs, a royalty of two and one-half percent (2½%) of Member's Price will be paid.

(l) On a sale of the right to publish the Work in English outside of the United States, or the right to translate the Work and publish it in other languages, fifty percent (50%) of the Publisher's receipts.

(m) On a sale of First Serial rights to the Work, the Author shall receive fifty percent (50%) of Publisher's receipts, except that on a sale of any serialization or excerpt from the Work to one of the Publisher's own periodicals, the Author shall receive one hundred percent (100%) of the fee paid for such a use.

(n) On a sale of the right of Second Serialization, the Author shall receive fifty percent (50%) of Publisher's receipts, except that in the case of a sale of Second Serial rights to one of the Publisher's own periodicals, the Author shall receive one hundred percent (100%) of the fee paid for such a use.

(o) The Publisher may permit others to reprint selections from the Work in textbooks, or with the Author's approval, in anthologies, and the Author shall receive fifty percent (50%) of the Publisher's receipts.

(p) If, before or after publication of the Work proper, the Publisher deems that part of the Work is salable as a separate book or booklet, it shall request of the Author such editorial changes as may be necessary to make this possible, and the terms of this Agreement, with the exception of Paragraphs 4(a) and 11(a), shall apply to this publication as if it were a new and separate work.

(q) If any part of the Work is included in an anthology published by the Publisher, the Author shall receive a fee to be negotiated between Author and Publisher.

(r) On bulk sales of the Work or any part of the Work for use as premiums or promotions, a royalty of ten percent (10%) of net receipts.

(s) On a license, with the Author's approval, for products or novelties based on the Work, or taking their name from the Work, the monies received shall be divided as follows: ninety percent (90%) to Author and ten percent (10%) to Publisher.

(t) The Publisher shall confer with the Author as to the nature, timing, and division of proceeds of any adaptation of the Work to be published by the Publisher or by others.

(u) Audiovisual or audio recording rights to the Work: If such rights are exercised by the Publisher, the Author shall receive ten percent (10%) of the Publisher's net receipts; if such rights are licensed, fifty percent (50%) of the Publisher's receipts.

(v) A royalty of fifty percent (50%) of Publisher's net receipts for granting to others any of Publisher's rights with respect to the Work hereunder not specified in Sub-paragraphs (a) through (u) above.

12. ROYALTY-FREE PROVISIONS

(a) No royalty shall be paid on free copies of the Work furnished to the Author or to others for purposes of review, sample, or similar purposes, or on damaged copies sold at or below manufacturing cost, or on copies which are destroyed by the Publisher.

(b) The Publisher shall have the right to permit others to publish or broadcast over radio or television selections from the Work without royalty, if the Publisher determines that such publication or broadcast will benefit sales of the Work. And the Publisher may use photographs or illustrations from the Work to promote or advertise the Work without making any payment to the Author.

(c) The Publisher is authorized to permit publication of the Work in Braille, or other reproduction of the Work for the physically handicapped without payment of fees and without compensation to the Author, providing no compensation is received by the Publisher.

(d) The Publisher may grant permission to publish extracts of the Work containing not more than five hundred (500) words, without compensation to Author or Publisher.

13. NOTICE OF LICENSE AGREEMENTS

The Publisher shall promptly furnish to the Author copies of any agreements in which the Publisher grants a license or other rights in the Work to others where the Author's share of the proceeds therefrom is, or in the Publisher's judgment is estimated to be, five hundred dollars ($500) or more.

14. FREE COPIES

Upon publication, the Publisher shall deliver to the Author twelve (12) free copies of the hardcover edition of the Work, twelve (12) free copies of any paperback edition of the Work published by the Publisher, and six (6) free copies of each substantially revised edition.

15. COPIES PURCHASED BY AUTHOR

The Publisher shall sell to the Author copies of any edition of the Work for resale or other purposes in quantities of less than 200 copies, at a discount of forty percent (40%) from the Publisher's list price; in single-order nonreturnable quantities of 200 or more copies, at a discount of forty-six percent (46%) from the Publisher's list price; and in single-order nonreturnable quantities of 1,000 or more copies, at a discount of fifty percent (50%) from the Publisher's list price, FOB the Publisher's warehouse or bindery.

The Author's purchases of any edition of the Work, up to a total of one thousand dollars ($1,000.00), may be charged to the Author's royalty account upon request, as long as the advance has been earned back and the account is not in a negative balance.

16. STATEMENTS AND PAYMENTS TO AUTHOR

(a) After publication, the Publisher will render to the Author semiannual statements, including available copies of statements of sublicensees, on February 28 and August 31 of each year following the first publication of the Work, which shall show all payments due Author hereunder for the six-month period ending on the preceding December 31 and June 30, respectively, and the basis for the determination thereof. Payments due the Author as shown thereon shall accompany such statement.

(b) If in the opinion of the Publisher, it is likely that credits for returns in a following royalty period will exceed income from sales and subsidiary rights income in that royalty period, then the Publisher may withhold from payment a reserve not to exceed fifteen percent (15%).

(c) The Author or the Author's designated representative shall have the right, upon thirty (30) days notice to the Publisher, to examine the Publisher's books of account relating to the Work. Such examination shall be at the Author's cost unless any additional amount found to be due Author upon such audit shall exceed five percent (5%) of the amount due Author as originally determined by the Publisher, in which case such audit shall be at the Publisher's expense.

17. RIGHT OF TERMINATION BY AUTHOR

The Author, at his election, may terminate this Agreement in the event of any of the following, in the following manner:

(a) if the Work is not published within the time specified in Paragraph 7, by notice to the Publisher, effective six (6) months after receipt thereof by the Publisher, unless the Work is published prior to the expiration of such six-month period;

(b) if the Work is not for sale in at least one edition (including any revised edition or reprint edition) published by the Publisher or under license from the Publisher and, within six months after written demand by the Author, the Publisher or its licensee fails to offer it again for sale, then this Agreement shall terminate and all rights granted to the Publisher in it shall revert to the Author;

(c) if the Publisher fails to deliver the semiannual statements or make any of the payments provided for herein, by notice to the Publisher effective thirty (30) days after receipt thereof by the Publisher, unless the Publisher delivers such statements or makes such payments within thirty (30) days after receipt of such notice;

(d) if the Publisher shall become bankrupt or file a petition for an arrangement under the Federal Bankruptcy Acts, or if it shall make a general assignment for the benefit of creditors, or if a trustee or a receiver shall be appointed of all or substantially all of the Publisher's assets, or if the Publisher shall take advantage of any insolvency law of any state of the United States, or shall commence the liquidation of its business, then immediately upon the happening of any of the said events, upon written notice by the Author to the Publisher, the Publisher's rights under this Agreement shall terminate.

18. EFFECT OF TERMINATION

Upon the effective date of the termination of this Agreement by the Author, or as soon thereafter as possible:

(a) The Publisher shall reassign to the Author all rights granted to the Publisher hereunder, with the exception of licenses theretofore granted. After such reversion, the Publisher shall continue to participate to the extent set forth in this Agreement in any license previously granted by it.

(b) The Author shall have the option to purchase the printing materials from the Publisher, if available from the printer, at the cost of retrieval and shipping, and any or all of the remaining sheets or copies of the Work at a price not to exceed the manufacturing cost. If the Author shall not have exercised his option to acquire such printing materials, sheets, or copies within sixty (60) days of the effective date of such termination, the Publisher shall have the right to destroy or to sell such remaining materials at cost or less, without payment to the Author on such sales, except as provided in Paragraph 11(u) of this Agreement.

(c) All accounts between the Author and the Publisher shall be adjusted and paid, except for any unearned advances.

19. INTERPRETATION

This Agreement shall be interpreted under the laws of the State of Ohio and of the United States of America.

20. ASSIGNMENT

Except as provided below, neither party may assign his or its rights or obligations in this Agreement or any portion thereof without the consent of the other:

(a) The Author may assign and transfer any monies due or to become due under this Agreement.

(b) The Publisher shall have the right to assign the Work to its own subsidiary or affiliated companies, and to authorize and sublicense publication or use of the Work throughout the world as set forth in Paragraphs 1 and 11 of this Agreement.

21. WAIVER

Failure by either party to promptly enforce any of his or its rights hereunder shall not constitute a waiver of those or any other rights or of strict compliance by the other party of its obligations hereunder, or in any way affect any other terms or conditions hereof.

22. MODIFICATION

No waiver, modification, or amendment to this Agreement shall be valid or enforceable unless it is in writing, signed by the parties.

23. ARBITRATION

Any controversy or claim arising out of this Agreement or the breach thereof shall be settled by arbitration in Cincinnati, Ohio, in accordance with the then-effective rules of the American Arbitration Association. The decision of the arbitrator(s) shall be binding upon the parties, and judgment thereon may be entered in any court of competent jurisdiction.

The Author has the right to refuse arbitration in case of the Publisher's failure to pay royalties, and to pursue other legal remedies in such a case.

24. NOTICES

Any notice required or permitted under this Agreement shall be in writing and delivered in person or by ordinary mail to the parties at their respective addresses set forth above, or to any other address as changed by notice in writing; provided, however, that notices of termination shall be delivered in person or by certified mail, return receipt requested.

25. FIRST REFUSAL

The Author hereby grants to the Publisher the right of first refusal to publish his next

on terms not less favorable than those contained in a bona fide offer to publish tendered to the Author by any third party. The Publisher shall exercise such right by notifying the Author of whether or not it wishes to publish said Work not later than twenty-one (21) days after receipt by Publisher of the manuscript or proposal/outline and sample chapters that represent the Author's next

26. AGENT

All sums due the Author under this Agreement shall be payable to the Author's agent, and shall be sent to such agent at the address indicated on Page One of this Agreement. The delivery of such sums to such agent shall be a full and valid discharge of the Publisher's obligations herein.

27. BINDING EFFECT

This Agreement shall be binding upon and inure to the benefit of the respective heirs, personal representatives, successors, and assigns of the parties.

IN WITNESS whereof, the parties hereto have executed this Agreement in duplicate on the date and year first above written.

AUTHOR:

WRITER'S DIGEST BOOKS
(A Division of F&W Publications, Inc.)

_____   By _____

_____
Social Security or Federal ID Number

APPENDIX F

Resources for Finding Agents and Publishers

PROFESSIONAL ASSOCIATIONS

If you send a SASE, the following writers' associations can provide lists of independent literary agents:

Society of Author's Representatives
39½ Washington Square Station
New York, NY 10012

Independent Literary Agents Association
% Ellen Levine Literary Agency
432 Park Ave. South
New York, NY 10016

RESOURCE BOOKS

The following is the most comprehensive list of names and addresses of literary agents in North America:

Literary Agents of North America
Published by Arthur Orrmont
Author Aid/Research Associates International
340 East 52nd Street
New York, NY 10022

The following provide names of publishers, editors, and agents throughout the U.S. Both books include short descriptions of the kinds of manuscripts each publisher is seeking. In *Writer's*

Market, other information, such as the names of editors to whom you should address your manuscript or proposal, and the advances one might expect, are also given for many publishing houses.

Literary Market Place
The Directory of American Book Publishing
R.R. Bowker Co., New York

Writer's Market
Where To Sell What You Write
Writer's Digest Books
Cincinnati, Ohio

BIBLIOGRAPHY

The following are books you may find helpful in putting together your writing collaboration.

The Author's Handbook, Franklynn Peterson and Judi Kesselman-Turkel. Englewood Cliffs, N. J.: Prentice-Hall, 1982.

The Complete Guide to Writing Nonfiction, The American Society of Journalists and Authors, edited by Glen Evans. Cincinnati: Writer's Digest Books, 1983.

Coping With Difficult People, Robert Bramson, New York: Ballantine 1985.

The Craft of Writing, William Sloan. New York: Ballantine 1984.

The Elements of Style, 3rd edition, William Strunk, Jr. and E. B. White, New York: Macmillan Publishing Co., Inc., 1979.

Getting Published: A Guide for Businesspeople and Other Professionals, Gary S. Belkin. New York: John Wiley & Sons, 1984.

How to Be Your Own Literary Agent, Richard Curtis. Boston: Houghton Mifflin Co., 1983.

How to Get Happily Published: A Complete and Candid Guide, Judith Appelbaum and Nancy Evans. New York: New American Library, 1982.

How to Sell What You Write, Jane Adams. New York: G. P. Putnam's Sons, 1984.

How to Understand and Negotiate a Book Contract or Magazine Article, Richard Balkin. Cincinnati: Writer's Digest Books, 1985.

How to Write a Book Proposal, Michael Larsen. Cincinnati: Writer's Digest Books, 1985.

How to Write a Winning Proposal, Oscar Collier. New York: American Writer's Corporation, 1982.

Literary Agents: How to Get & Work With the Right One for You, Michael Larsen. Cincinnati: Writer's Digest Books, 1986.

Literary Market Place: The Directory of American Book Publishing, New York: R. R. Bowker Co., 1985.

Max Perkins: Editor of Genius, A. Scott Berg, New York: Pocket Books, 1978.

The One Minute Manager, Kenneth Blanchard and Spencer Johnson. New York: William Morrow, 1982.

A Writer's Guide to Book Publishing, 2nd edition, Richard Balkin. New York: Hawthorn/Dutton, 1981.

Writer's Market (updated annually), Cincinnati: Writer's Digest Books.

INDEX